TEACH YOURSELF
Bluegrass Guitar

by Russ Barenberg

Teach yourself authentic bluegrass. Clear instructions from a professional; basics, right- and left-hand techniques, solos, backup, personal advice on performance, and much more. Plus a complete selection of the best bluegrass songs and tunes to learn from.

Project editors: Peter Pickow and Ed Lozano
Musical contractor: Bob Grant
Interior design and layout: Don Giller

This book Copyright © 1978 by Amsco Publications,
A Division of Music Sales Corporation, New York
This edition published 1999 by Oak Publications,
A Division of Embassy Music Corporation, New York

PLAYBACK+
Speed • Pitch • Balance • Loop

To access audio visit:
www.halleonard.com/mylibrary

Enter Code
5867-0744-8772-7566

ISBN 978-0-8256-0325-9

Visit Hal Leonard Online at
www.halleonard.com

Contact us:
Hal Leonard
7777 West Bluemound Road
Milwaukee, WI 53213
Email: info@halleonard.com

In Europe, contact:
Hal Leonard Europe Limited
42 Wigmore Street
Marylebone, London, W1U 2RN
Email: info@halleonardeurope.com

In Australia, contact:
Hal Leonard Australia Pty. Ltd.
4 Lentara Court
Cheltenham, Victoria, 3192 Australia
Email: info@halleonard.com.au

Audio Track Listing

Personnel

Bob Grant: Guitar, Mandolin, and Vocals
Tony Trischka: Banjo
Antoine Silverman: Fiddle
Matt Weiner: Bass

Table of Contents

Introduction

This book will get you acquainted with many of the standard songs and instrumentals in the bluegrass repertoire as it teaches you the details of bluegrass guitar playing. You'll find interesting guitar breaks for all of the tunes, and backup parts for several of them. All the parts of each song, including the melody, are written in tablature so that you don't have to know how to read music to use the book.

For beginners, I've included simple and complete instruction of the basics of backup and lead playing that will prepare you for learning the tunes. There are a fair number of easy songs to get you started. If you've already played some bluegrass you can use the book as a valuable source of songs and solos and as an enjoyable means of refining your playing. The guitar parts gradually increase in difficulty, and they get pretty fancy by the end of the book. There you'll be introduced to some advanced techniques and modern styles of bluegrass and newgrass playing.

Tips on how to turn the tablature into good bluegrass will enrich your feel for the music as you learn which notes to play. In addition, there's information about what to play and when to play it in a bluegrass band so you'll have a better idea of what to do when you get together with other pickers.

One nice feature of this book is that the tunes can also be found in an Everybody's Favorite book for each of the other bluegrass instruments. So if you have friends who play the fiddle, banjo, mandolin, or bass, you can try playing these tunes in a group. Even if you can't get together a complete bluegrass band, it's always fun to try out what you've learned with others. Just playing with one other person can do wonders for your sense of time and will help draw you into the spirit of the music.

Be sure to study carefully the section on reading tablature so that you understand the rhythmic notation before you start to learn the music. For each of the tunes, the melody is written in tablature on the upper staff, and the break is on the lower one. On some tunes, a backup part is given along with the melody, which is above it. These parts are presented before the breaks. Once you've learned the backup parts, you should have no trouble playing rhythm guitar to any other bluegrass songs as long as you know the chords.

On the songs, you might want to learn the melody and chords first so you can hum the tune, strum along, and get familiar with it. Then, when you learn the break you'll see how it relates to and embellishes the melody. On instrumentals it might be best to learn the breaks first. (The melody line is often very similar to the break, particularly in some of the fiddle tunes.) Once you know a break, try to find someone to play backup and accompany you so that you can hear the chord changes as you play.

Learn the tunes first in the key they are written without using a capo. If you're going to play with people who are learning from the other Teach Yourself bluegrass books, put your capo on the fret specified at the beginning of that particular tune. This will put you in the right key. However, only some of the tunes require a capo.

Try to listen to as much bluegrass as you can to get a feel for how these tunes can sound. I have included a discography at the back of the book. I hope you have a great time learning and playing the music.

Reading Tablature

A tablature staff has six lines that represent the strings of a guitar. The low E string is on the bottom.

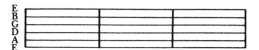

Numbers written on the lines indicate which fret to play on each string. A C chord would look like this:

Rhythmic Notation and Keeping Time

Vertical lines across the staff divide the tablature into small sections called measures.

The time signature is indicated on the first line of tablature for each tune. It tells you how many beats are in each measure. All but two of the songs in this book are written in 4/4 time. In 4/4 time there are always four quarter notes (beats) per measure. When you are learning the tunes, count one-two-three-four for the quarter notes in every measure and tap your foot on each count. Play these quarter notes on the open G string:

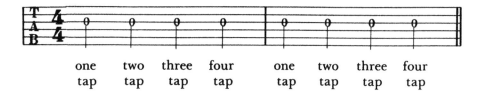

3/4 Time

Willow Garden and *All the Good Times Are Past and Gone* are the two tunes I mentioned that are not in 4/4/ time. They are in 3/4 or "waltz" time. In 3/4 time there are three beats or quarter notes per measure. Be sure to count and play evenly at a moderate pace so that all the notes are of the same length and there are no pauses between measures.

A note that lasts for only half a beat is called an eighth note, so two of them are equivalent to one quarter note. If you count one-and-two-and-three-and-four-and for each measure, you are counting eighth notes. One falls on the beat as you tap your foot, and the next falls off the beat as you lift between taps:

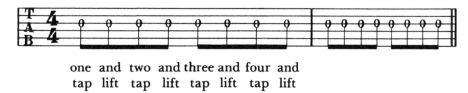

Eighth notes can be written in groups of four as they are above, but they also appear singly and in pairs:

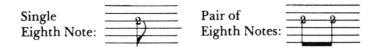

No matter how they are written, each one always has the same rhythmic value (half a beat) within a particular tune.

A note that lasts for two beats (the duration of two quarter notes) is called a half note, and in tablature it is written with no flag. It appears on the staff as simply a number:

one   two   three   four   one   two   three   four

When two of the same notes are tied by an arch (⌒), you play only the first one but add them both together to make one longer note:

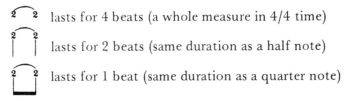

Note: Ties (⌒) used to connect two different notes in the melody tablature are called slurs and mean only that you sing both of those notes on the same syllable of the lyrics.

Triplet rhythms are used in a couple of tunes in this book. A triplet divides a quarter note into three equal parts and is indicated like this:

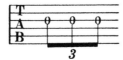

You play three evenly spaced notes in the span of one quarter note. They are not eighth notes even though they are written with eighth note flags; they're actually slightly faster than eighth notes.

Always remember to keep the beat constant when you are counting or playing. Never leave uncalled-for gaps between notes; this causes breaks in the rhythm.

Rests

Pauses between notes are indicated by rests:

- ▬ rest (pause) for a whole measure
- ▬ rest for two beats (duration of one half note)
- 𝄽 rest for one beat (duration of one quarter note)
- 𝄾 rest for half a beat (duration of one eighth note)

Be sure to continue your normal counting through the rests so that time is kept correctly.

When you're learning the guitar parts in the book you'll probably be playing at a slower tempo at first and tapping a beat for every quarter note (four per measure) as we have done so far. However, when you finally play a bluegrass tune up to tempo, you will feel the actual pulse (foot taps) most naturally on each half note; then tap your foot only twice in each measure and play the equivalent of two quarter notes or four eighth notes for each tap.

Some other symbols

Numbers above the tablature staff indicate left-hand fingerings (1 is the index finger, etc.). These are only included when there might be some doubt about how to finger a passage. Alternate fingerings are sometimes given in parentheses.

> This sign over a note indicates an accent or added emphasis on that note.

⊓ Down-stroke of the pick.

V Up-stroke of the pick.

|: :| These are repeat signs. If a section of music is bounded by these signs, repeat that section once, then go on.

These signs indicate first and second endings to a repeated section of music. When you come to them, play only the first ending. Then repeat the section indicated. This time, skip the first ending and play the second one. Then go on.

Rules of Pick Direction

Pick direction won't be indicated (except as an occasional reminder) unless it deviates from the following rules:

1) Use a down-stroke on notes that start on the first eighth note of each beat (on the beats).
2) Use an up-stroke on notes that start on the second eighth note of each beat (on the off-beats).

Therefore, an uninterrupted string of eighth notes will always be played with a steady back and forth motion of the pick. Any note written as a half note or a quarter note gets a down-stroke. Here's an example of a fairly complicated passage and how to pick it. Refer to it later if you have any questions about figuring out pick direction.

Using a Flatpick

Nowadays, bluegrass guitar is almost always played with a flatpick. Some players (such as Lester Flatt) achieve a fine rhythm guitar sound using a thumbpick and their fingers. But if you're interested in playing runs and solos, a flatpick is a must. Ideally you'd want to use a large-bodied, flat-top steel string guitar for bluegrass flatpicking. But don't feel you have to run out and buy one. The guitar you have will probably be just fine on which to learn.

Picks come in many shapes, sizes and colors. Feel free to experiment with different ones until you find something that feels comfortable, works well and goes with your shirt. I suggest using either a medium or (better yet) a heavy gauge pick. A stiffer pick will allow you to get more sound out of the instrument with a better tone and less pick noise. It may feel awkward at first, but with a less pliable pick, you will soon develop a feeling of more direct and controlled contact with the string.

I've seen several different ways of holding a flatpick that can work well. So if you already play and feel comfortable with a method other than mine, don't feel you have to change (although you might want to give it a try). The style I describe here is definitely the most common and, I think, the most effective for playing an acoustic guitar in the bluegrass style.

Hold the flatpick securely between the flat part of your thumb and the side of the last section of your index finger. The index finger should be curled in the shape of the letter C. Only a small portion of the tip of the pick should be exposed for playing; the rest is held. Let the three other fingers of your right hand fall in a relaxed way. These fingers should never stiffen. Keep them in a loose, half-curled position, Rest your upper arm on the side of the guitar so that you are free to move at the elbow and so that the pick ends up in a position over the back half of the sound hole (toward the bridge). It's okay to let your hand drag loosely over the top and pickguard as you play. But don't pin your fingers down rigidly on the top and pivot from them.

Now finger a G chord and strum slowly across all of the strings. If it feels like you're about to lose your grip, hold the pick more securely, but be careful not to squeeze so tightly that you feel cramped and tense. Try for a firm grip on the pick while your hand and arm are relaxed.

Left-hand Tips

For a good, clean sound and accurate fingering, keep the fingers of your left hand arched so that they come down squarely on the string at almost a right angle to the fingerboard. Whether you're playing a chord or a single note, put each finger as close as you can to the fret being played without putting it directly on top of the fret. This allows you to play with less pressure and helps eliminate buzzy notes, which tend to occur when your finger is too far behind the fret.

Basic Rhythm Guitar Playing

In bluegrass music, the guitar was originally used almost entirely for rhythm. Along with the bass, it provided a solid yet lively foundation that supported the melodic instruments and the voices. Nowadays it's becoming more and more common for the guitar to participate as a lead instrument. However, maintaining rhythm is still its primary function. Good backup playing can really make a big difference in the overall sound of a bluegrass band.

Bluegrass rhythm guitar playing is all centered around a repeated picking pattern. It consists of a single bass note followed by a strummed chord, and it sounds like "boom-chink." For example, finger a G chord and play:

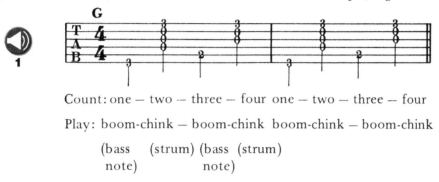

Count: one — two — three — four one — two — three — four

Play: boom-chink — boom-chink boom-chink — boom-chink

     (bass   (strum) (bass (strum)
     note)   note)

Note: use this fingering for G whenever possible:

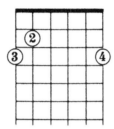

Within each chord, the bass note generally alternates back and forth between two notes. You can refer to the following tablature to see which bass notes to play in the chords most commonly found in bluegrass. As you learn the backup parts, you'll get a good sense of how to choose the bass notes:

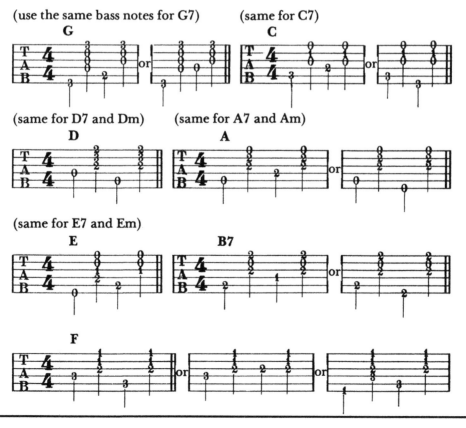

When you play the boom-chink pattern, pick the bass notes firmly and let them ring for two beats (even though in tablature they're written as quarter notes for convenience). Aim for control when you play single notes. Don't slap at the strings from too great a distance with too broad a motion.

When you strum, brush across the three or four upper strings with an even sound. Be sure to stay loose at the wrist and elbow when you flatpick. Feel your arm swing from the elbow while you control the exact moment of picking the string(s) with your wrist. In order to produce a good sound and a snappy rhythm, your arm should be relaxed and free to move. This will help you avoid overly loud and clunky strums. Ham-handedness will not lead to fame and fortune in the bluegrass world. On the other hand, don't be bashful. Bluegrass is pretty loud music, and to be effectively heard along with the banjo, fiddle, and mandolin, you can't afford to play too softly. Although it may feel awkward at first when you're struggling to control the pick and hit the right strings, you'll soon be able to produce a strong, clear sound and still feel your arm and hand are relaxed. The backup part for *Roll in My Sweet Baby's Arms* makes use of simple boom-chink playing.

A variation of the boom-chink pattern is shown below for a C chord:

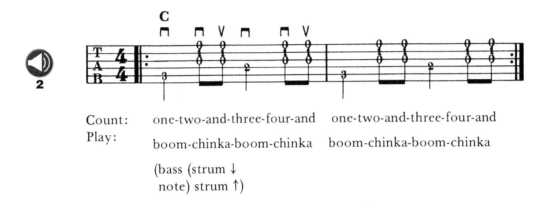

Count: one-two-and-three-four-and   one-two-and-three-four-and
Play: boom-chinka-boom-chinka   boom-chinka-boom-chinka

      (bass (strum ↓
      note) strum ↑)

This is probably the most common way to play bluegrass backup. Here you play a bass note followed by a double strum, down and back. The up-strum need not contain more than two or three notes. For a good sound, try to use a relaxed swinging motion as you strum down and back. Don't be stiff.

Here's another variation to keep you from falling asleep at the pick. It sounds like "boompa-chinka" and is shown for a D chord:

You play a small up-strum between the bass note and the down-strum. It should contain only one or two notes, usually from among the D, G, and B strings. This pattern produces a rolling continuous effect and sounds good with an accent on the back beat (down-strum). Again, let the bass notes ring for two beats.

As you practice your backup playing, don't get hung up on trying to hit the exact number of strings indicated for the strums. Aim first for a smooth, full sound, a solid beat, and an even rhythm.

The three variations you've learned can all be used within a song and can even be combined within a single measure. Once you feel comfortable playing all of these variations, follow your musical impulses in deciding which to use and how to combine them in a particular song. For some reason it's usually best to combine the boompa-chinka pattern so that one of the others precedes it in a measure. For example:

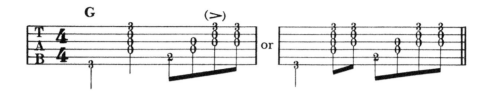

You can practice playing the variations in place in a simple boom-chink in the backup part for *Roll in My Sweet Baby's Arms*.

3/4 Time

For tunes in 3/4 time the basic rhythm guitar pattern in each measure is one bass note followed by two strums down and back. Finger an A chord and play:

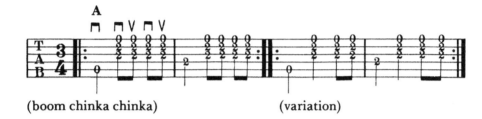

(boom chinka chinka)   (variation)

Bass Runs

After you've gotten a feel for the fundamentals of bluegrass, you can start to make your playing more interesting and more musical. Learning bass runs is the first step.

A bass run is a series of single bass notes that usually lead from one chord to another. Sometimes they're played while one chord is held. Here are some runs from G to C and from C back to G:

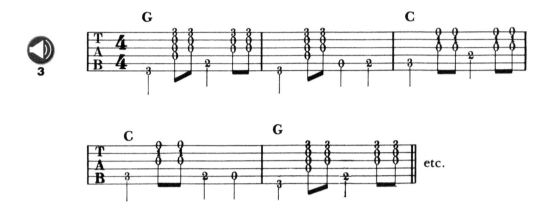

Other simple runs are included in the backup parts to *John Hardy, Soldier's Joy* and *All the Good Times Are Past and Gone.*

The runs you'll learn throughout this book are common, but they are by no means the only ones. Play as much as you can, and before you know it you'll be able to make up and even improvise your own runs.

Here are some pointers to help you make your runs sound good:

1) To insure that all the notes ring clearly, try to fret each one before you strike the string with your pick. By getting your left-hand finger down first, you can eliminate stubby notes caused by picking the string slightly before you have it fretted. Try to eliminate those gaps between the notes that are caused by sluggish fingering.

2) Pick with control and avoid slapping at the strings. You don't want to become one of those eager but sloppy players who seem to prefer hitting two strings when one would do.

3) Runs can really add movement to the music. So play them rhythmically and give them some life by emphasizing certain notes more than others.

On Rhythm Guitar and Playing with Other People

Whether you're playing guitar with just one other person or with a full bluegrass band, try to be aware of how your playing affects the music and of what you're contributing to the band sound. For example, sometimes you might want to emphasize the bass notes and bass runs so that they are heard more prominently, thereby giving an undercurrent of movement to the total sound. At other times you might choose to really hit the strums of the chords so that the back beat is stronger. Be aware of how you can control the feel of a song through these kinds of musical variations.

Bluegrass can be exciting music, but only if you play with spirit, expression and rhythmic drive. Pay attention to dynamics. You'll be more popular at parking lot picking sessions if you listen as much as possible to the other people in the band and don't play unresponsively at the same volume all the time. Try to notice the different rhythmic qualities of various bluegrass songs (bouncy, driving, flowing, etc.) and be sure to listen to recordings of good rhythm guitar players like Jimmy Martin, Clarence White, Peter Rowan, and many of the guitarists who have played with Bill Monroe over the years. Good backup playing need not contain a lot of fancy runs. Simple bass runs played solidly in the right placed can be very effective.

Simple Melodic Playing

There's a style of melodic country guitar playing that can be thought of as an extension of the rhythm guitar techniques you've just learned. Rather than playing alternating bass notes or bass runs, you play the melody of the song along with the accompanying strums in the treble strings. This is sometimes known as the Carter Family style, named after the famous musical family who used it in many of their songs back in the 1930s. It's a kind of solo playing commonly used in certain bluegrass songs, several of which are included in our first section of tunes. These breaks provide a good introduction to playing lead guitar and they're not much more difficult than bass runs.

In this style, a chord or part of a chord is usually held with the left hand as you pick the melody and strum. Move your fingers from the chord position only to play melodic notes not contained in the chord itself. Don't necessarily release the whole chord. The strums should be less forceful than they would be in backup playing. Once you get the notes, concentrate on making them sound good and smooth.

Here are a few techniques that are common in bluegrass. They are all methods of producing a note with your left hand without picking the string.

Hammer-On

After playing a note you bring down a finger of your left hand suddenly and firmly on a higher fret so that the string keeps ringing on the new note. For example:

Pull-Off

This is the opposite of a hammer-on. After playing a note, you pick the same string with your left hand by pulling your finger off the fret being played, which leaves a lower note ringing. The lower note can be either an open string or another fretted note.

As you pull your finger up and off the string, pull it slightly across in the direction of your palm to give the string a small pluck. Be careful not to hit the neighboring string (in this case, the D string).

Slides

After a note is picked, you produce the next one by quickly sliding your finger to another fret on the same string. Make sure the first note rings for its full rhythmic value before you slide to the next one.

You can also use a slide as a quick approach to the main note. This is indicated as follows:

You hear a fast slide that starts at the second fret, followed instantly by the note on the fourth fret that rings solidly on the first eighth note of the beat. There is not an actual note played at the second fret; it is only an indication of the slide's starting point. (This same effect can be achieved with a hammer-on.)

Now here are some tunes. Hope you enjoy them!

Roll in My Sweet Baby's Arms

5   6

Capo on 2nd fret:
actual Key of A

Back up

Verse

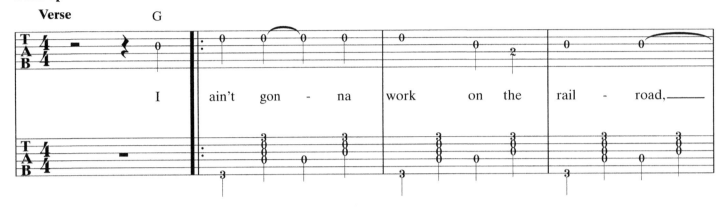

I ain't gon - na work on the rail - road,____

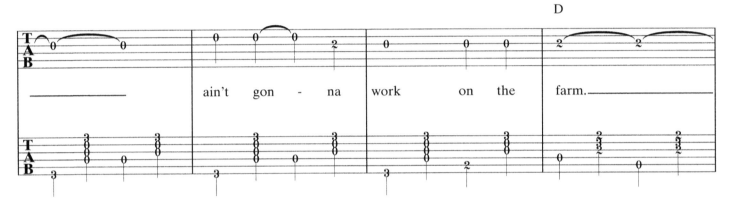

____ ain't gon - na work on the farm.____

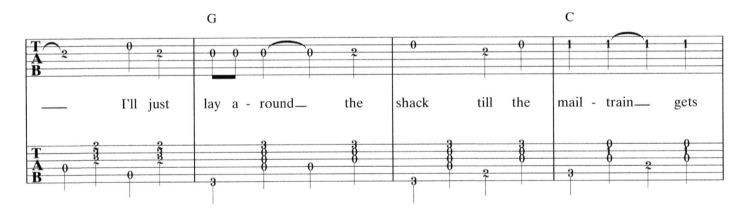

____ I'll just lay a - round__ the shack till the mail - train__ gets

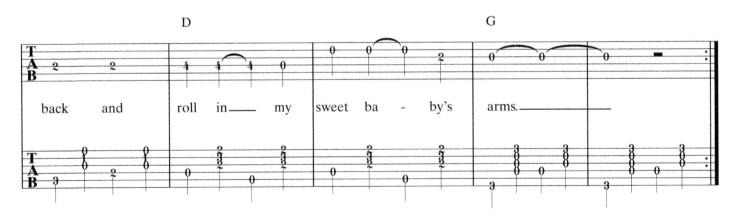

back and roll in__ my sweet ba - by's arms._____

Roll in My Sweet Baby's Arms

Break

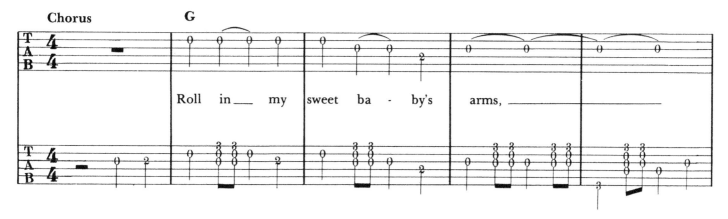

Chorus   **G**

Roll in __ my sweet ba - by's arms, _____

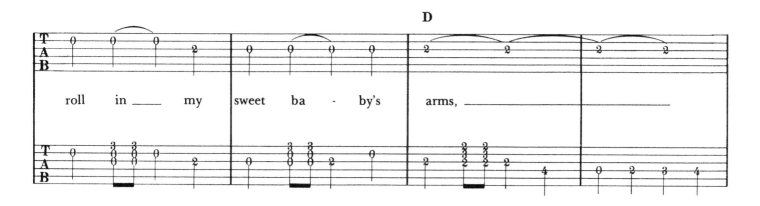

D

roll in __ my sweet ba - by's arms, _____

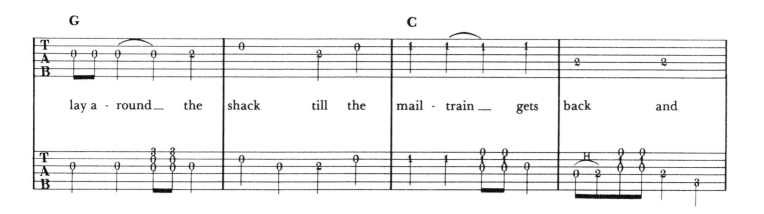

G   **C**

lay a - round __ the shack till the mail - train __ gets back and

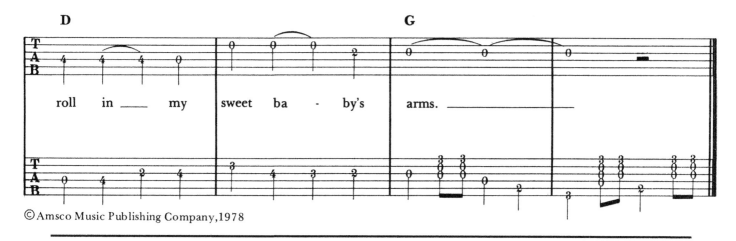

D   **G**

roll in __ my sweet ba - by's arms. _____

Will the Circle Be Unbroken

**Capo on 2nd fret:
actual Key of D**

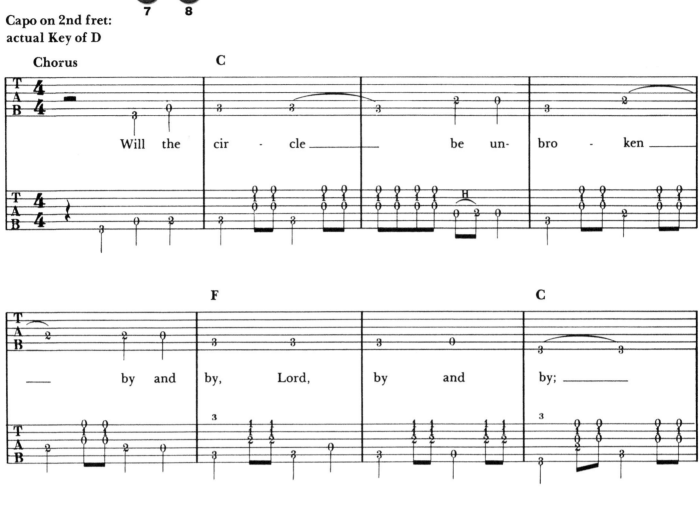

Will the cir - cle ____ be un- bro - ken ____

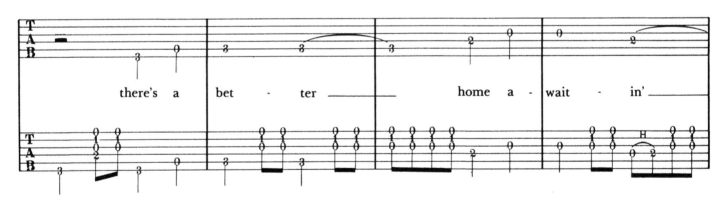

____ by and by, Lord, by and by; ____

____ there's a bet - ter ____ home a - wait - in'

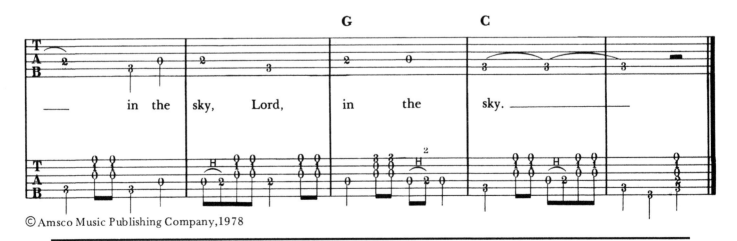

____ in the sky, Lord, in the sky. ____

Key of C

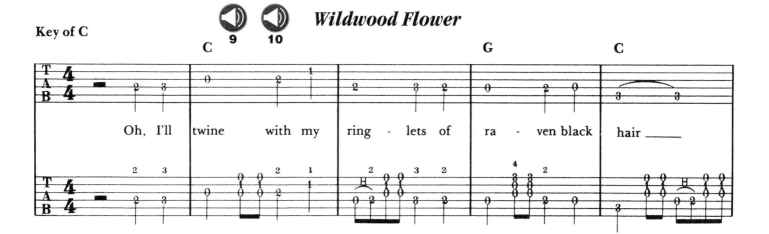

Oh, I'll twine with my ring - lets of ra - ven black hair ____

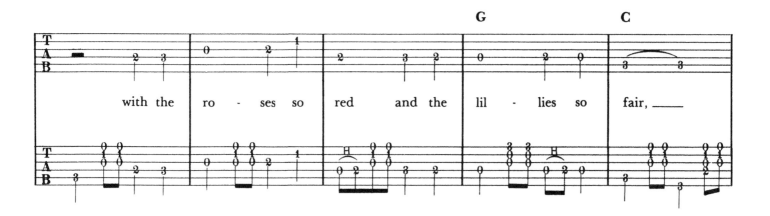

with the ro - ses so red and the lil - lies so fair, ____

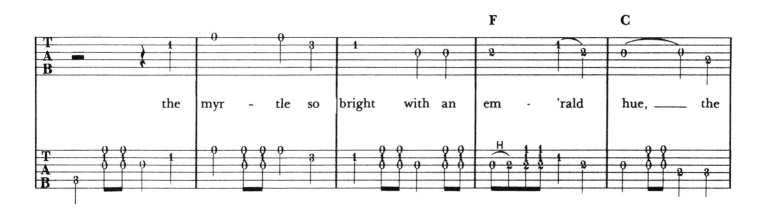

the myr - tle so bright with an em - 'rald hue, ____ the

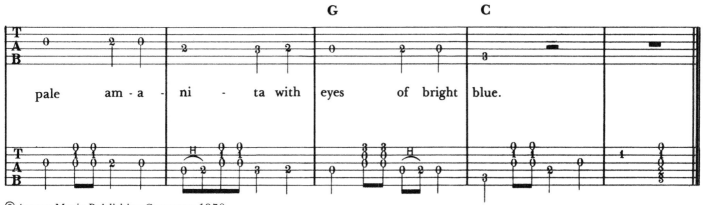

pale am - a - ni - ta with eyes of bright blue.

John Hardy

Backup
(with simple bass runs)

Key of G

John Hardy

Break

Key of G

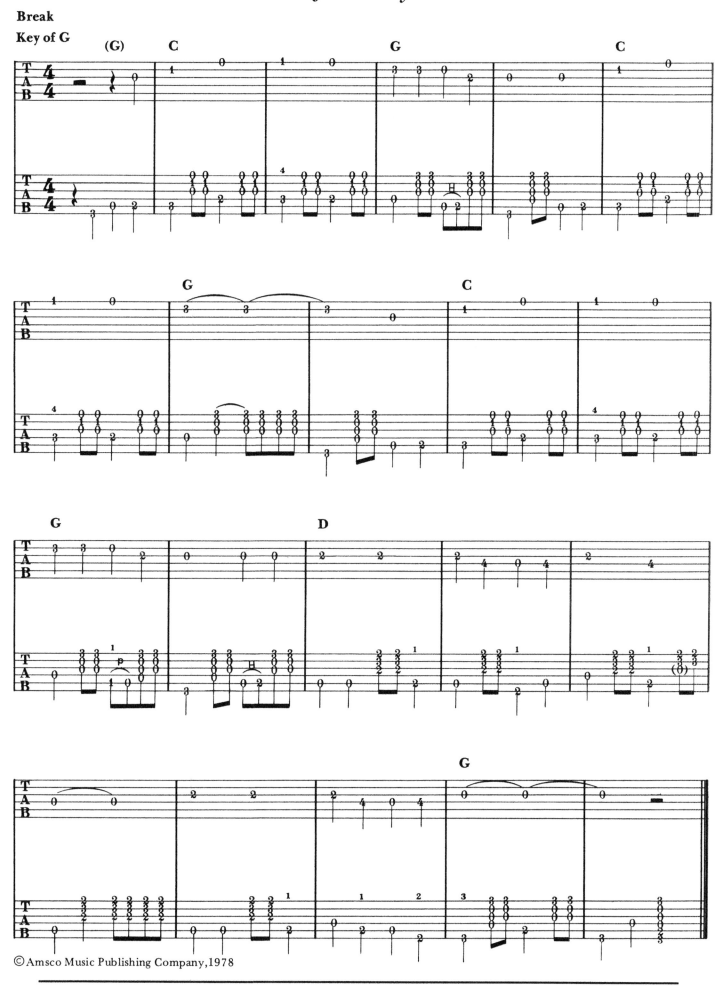

Key of C

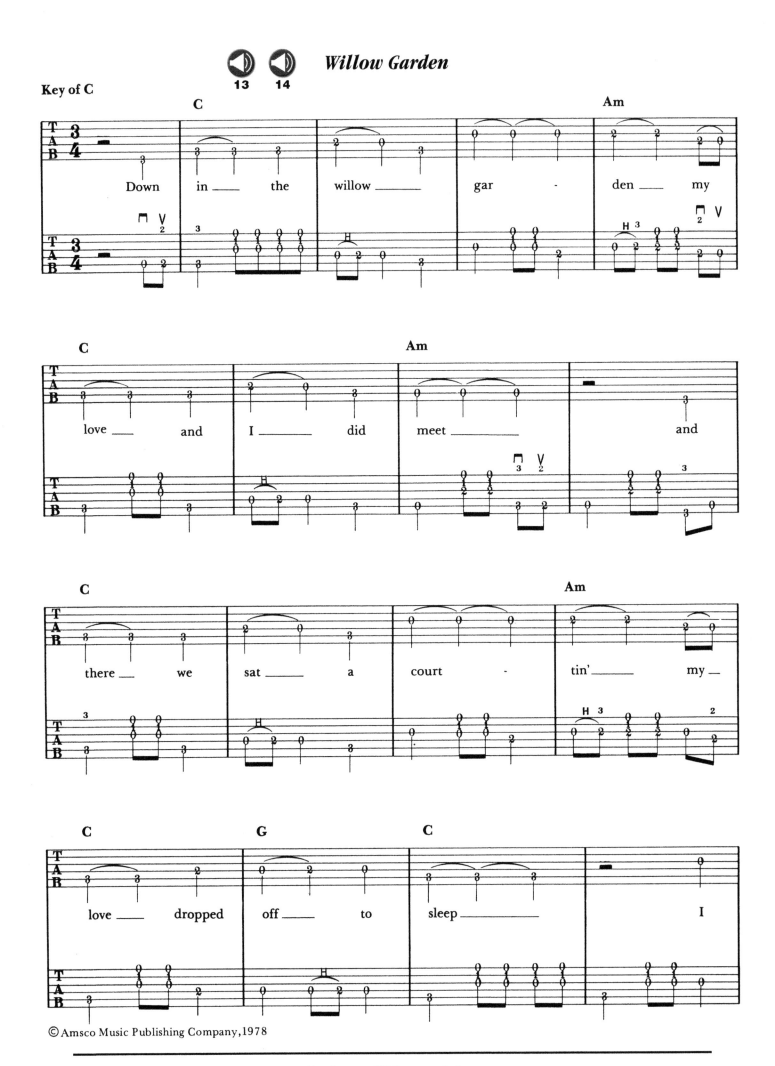

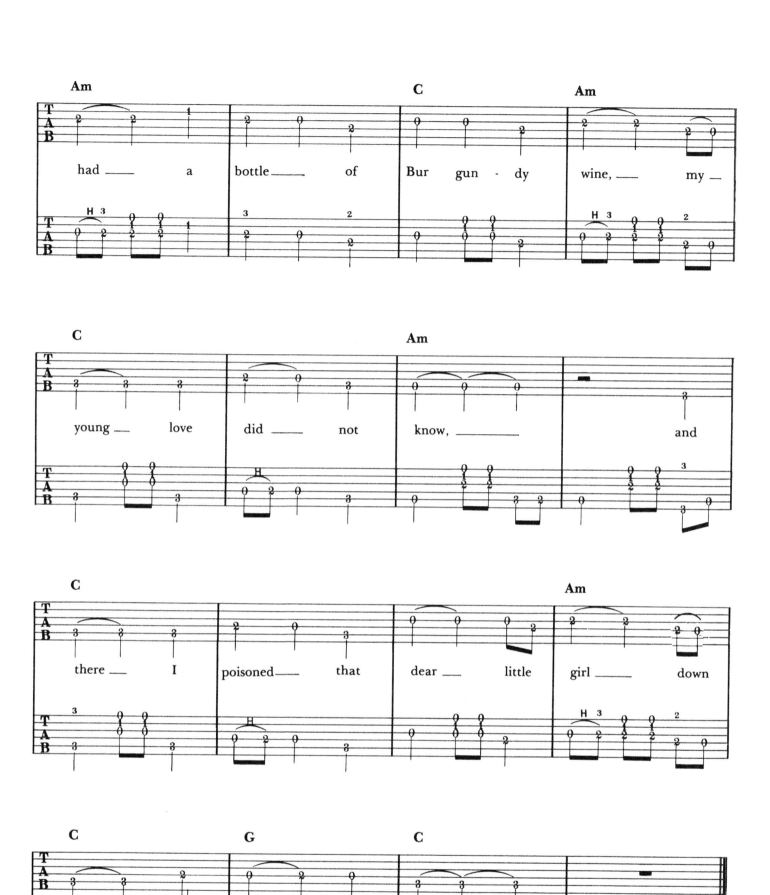

Under the Double Eagle

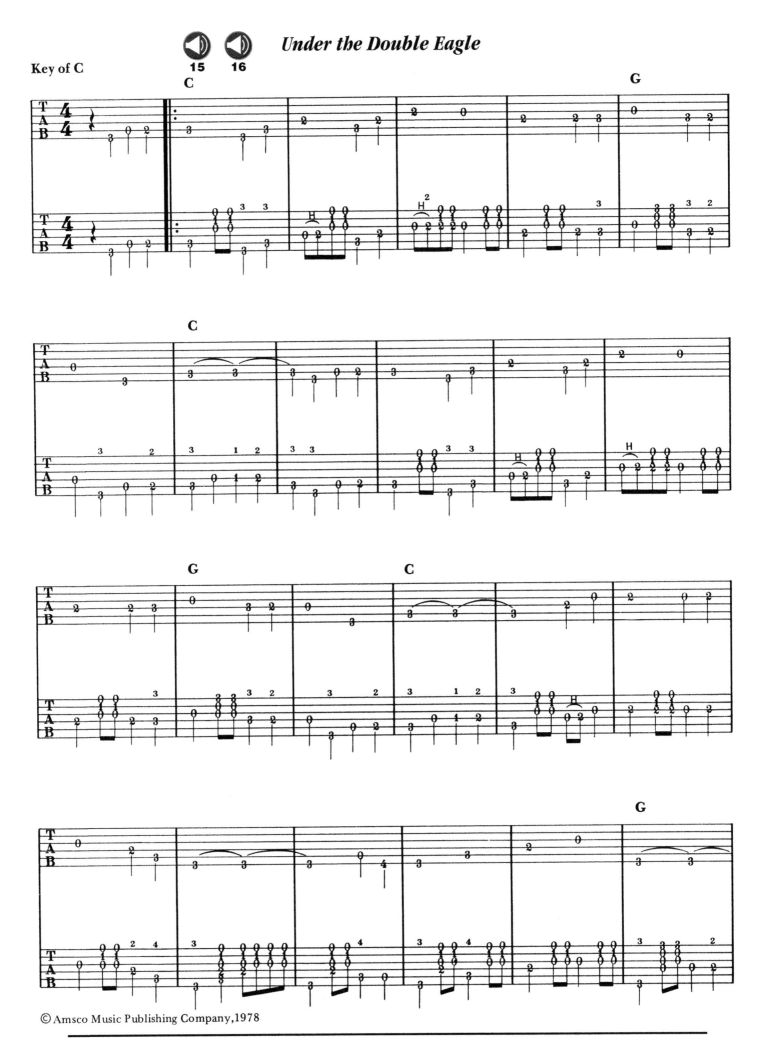

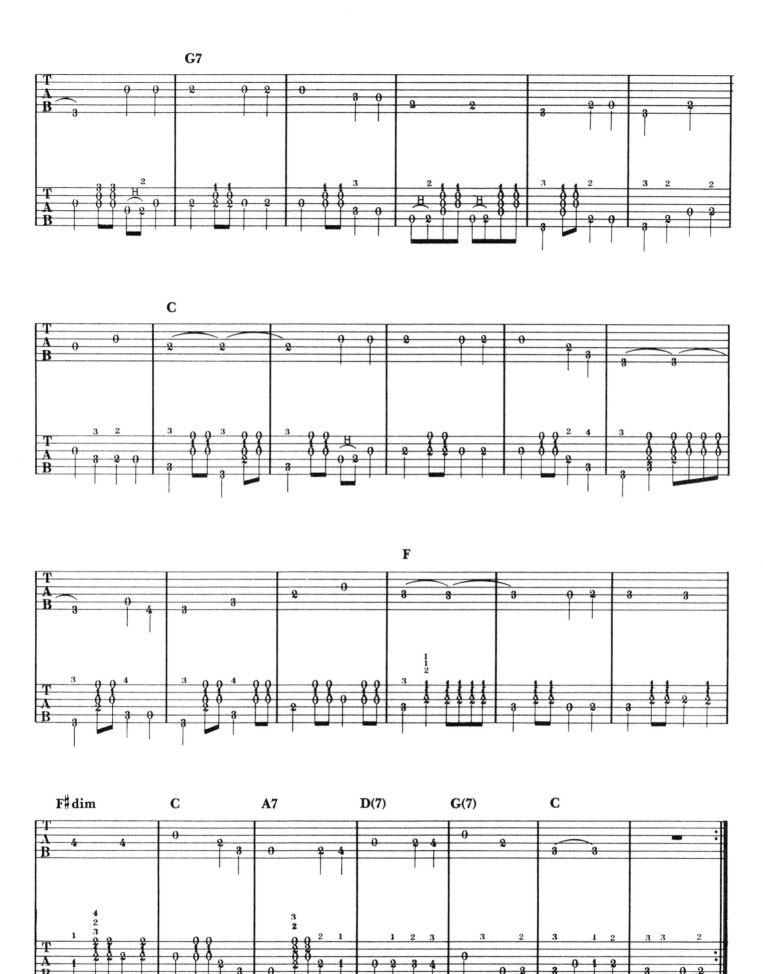

Capo on 2nd fret:
actual Key of A
Backup

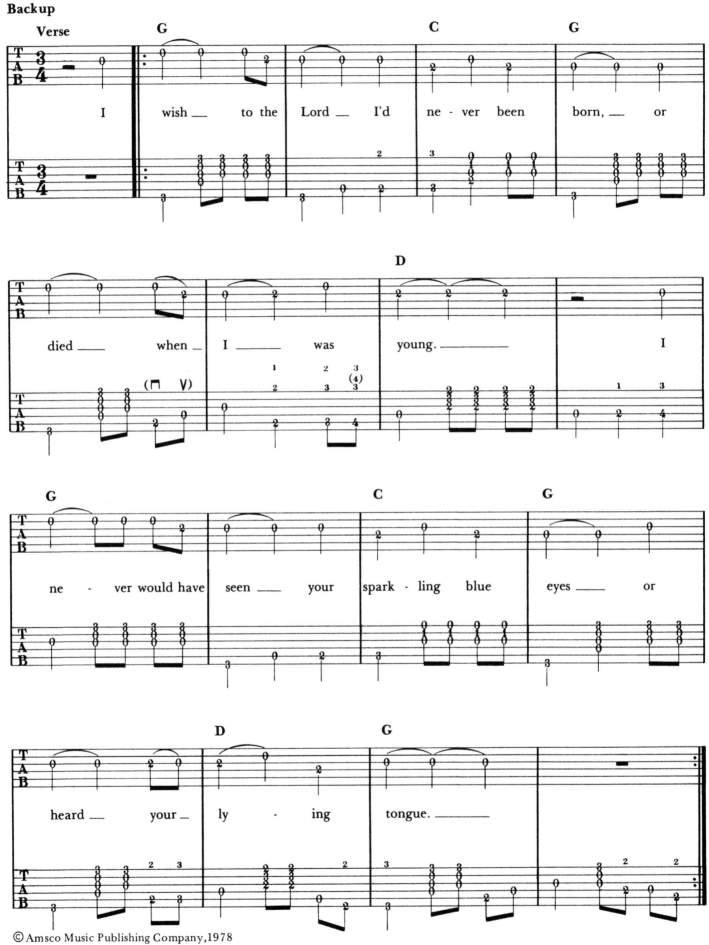

All the Good Times Are Past and Gone

Break

Lead Playing with an Alternating Pick Stroke

Most bluegrass guitar breaks involve laying single notes with a down and back motion of the pick that corresponds to the flow of eighth notes (as I described in the Rules of Pick Direction). This kind of picking occurs most straightforwardly in playing fiddle tunes such as *Old Joe Clark, Blackberry Blossom,* and *Fire on the Mountain.* Notice the basic connection between the down and up motion and the stronger and weaker notes in a measure. Down-strokes tend to feel a bit more solid. This is as it should be, since those notes fall on the beat. However, you should be able to play up-strokes with just as much control and volume so that every note in a string of eighth notes sounds even.

To avoid sloppiness, try to reduce the distance your pick moves. But stay relaxed and maintain the rhythmic feel of the swinging back and forth motion. Aim for a continuous, flowing sound, making sure the notes are cleanly fretted when you pick them. In general, let each note ring right up until the next one is played. Your left hand is no longer working off a chord position; rather, it is released to finger the single notes of the solo. Playing breaks is not easy, but soon your hands will start to cooperate with you, and it will feel relaxed and fluid.

Fiddle Tunes

A fiddle tune is one of the most common types of bluegrass instrumentals and often lends itself well to guitar breaks. Doc Watson was the first to popularize guitar versions of fiddle tunes. They usually have two parts (A and B), and each section is played twice (sometimes with different endings), so that the basic format of the tune is AABB. Most of the fiddle tunes in the next section are in a more or less straight-ahead style in the tradition of Doc Watson.

In any melody, certain notes get more emphasis than others. It's not hard to pick up the pulse of fiddle tunes and bluegrass songs. What will help you the most is listening to recordings and live performances. The beat is infectious and easy to get into your system.

Soloing on Songs

Solos on bluegrass songs are derived from the song's melody and should follow it to a large extent. Compared to a fiddle tune, which is characterized by a steady stream of notes, a song has a more drawn-out melody and longer and more frequent pauses between phrases. Therefore, these breaks often use more varied rhythms and contain extra notes and strums to embellish the melodies. The break to *Nine Pound Hammer* is a good example.

In songs that have a verse and chorus with different melodies, solos are given for both parts. A bluegrass song usually begins with an instrumental break and ends with a vocal chorus (or a verse, in songs with no chorus). In most arrangements, the other breaks are played after a chorus of singing. Here is a typical bluegrass arrangement:

Break-verse-chorus-break-verse-chorus-break-verse-chorus-end.

Flatt Runs and How to Use Them

When you see a live bluegrass band or listen to bluegrass recordings, you'll probably notice that the guitar players have a favorite run, particularly when they are playing a G chord. It's commonly referred to as the Flatt run, after Lester Flatt, who popularized it. Here is its basic form:

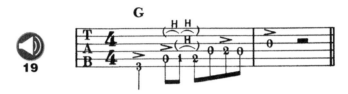

It's often played with a single or double hammer-on as shown above, but learn it with separate pick strokes as well. Give it a little bounce and observe the accents, especially the last one. (This note is the cause of many a broken G string.) The Flatt run is amazingly useful and has many variations, each with its own special charm. For the connoisseur, here are some of its other forms:

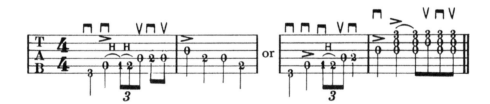

These runs have a very bluegrassy sound and are really effective in medium-to-fast songs with a strong beat. Be sure to put a big accent on the second note to give a lift to the run. Play the triplet quickly and evenly, fitting all three notes into the duration of a quarter note. The ending of the second version given above is a very useful strumming pattern for rhythm guitar playing.

Here's more:

Here's how Flatt runs are most commonly used:

1) Leading to a chord change. For example, in *Sitting on Top of the World,* it leads to the first C chord.

2) At the end of phrases, or in the gaps between phrases. For example, in *Sitting on Top of the World,* after ". . . and I don't worry . . .," and after the last line, ". . . cause I'm sittin' on top of the world. . . ."

3) At the beginning or end of a song.

A large number of bluegrass tunes are played in G position on the guitar. Though the runs I've discussed here are usually played in G, corresponding runs can be played on other chords:

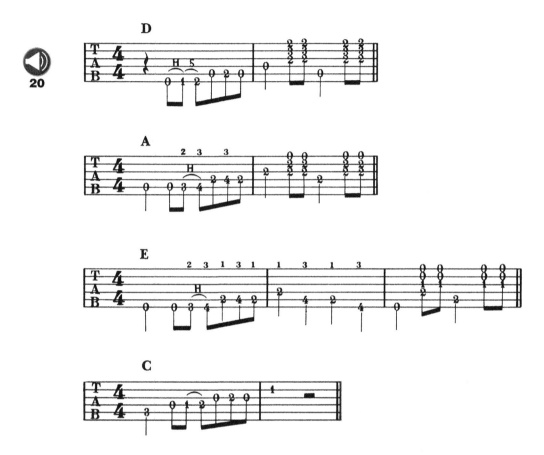

Beginning a Tune

Most songs and instrumentals begin with a lead-in lick by the instrument playing the opening solo. The rest of the band comes in on the downbeat of the break. For instance, if you are going to start off *Little Maggie,* here's how it might go:

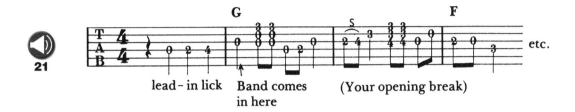

Lead-in licks for the guitar are included for the most of the solos in this book.

The Flatt run can be used to begin a song:

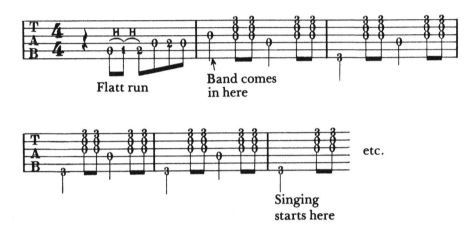

In this case there is no break at the beginning. After the run, the band comes in and there are four measures of rhythm playing, over which the banjo or fiddle might play a lick. The song then starts right in with the singing. Try this intro with a longer guitar run preceding the Flatt run:

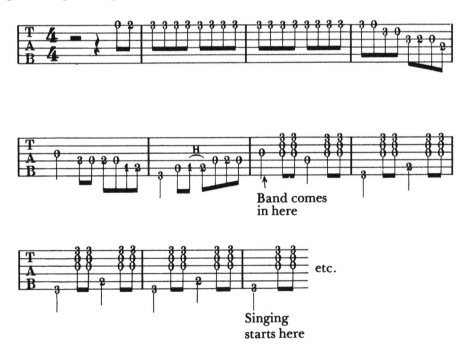

Instrumentals in which the banjo plays the opening break often start with a two-measure banjo lick followed by a Flatt run on the guitar, and then the beginning of the banjo solo.

Endings for Songs

Now I know you love to pick, but you've got to stop sometime. Here's one common way to end a bluegrass song. Play a Flatt run starting on the last note of the final chorus:

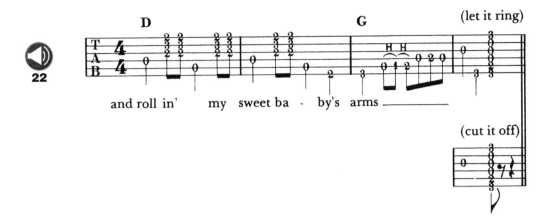

To cut off the final chord, damp the strings quickly with both hands. Avoid vicious arguments with fellow band members over whether to cut it off or let it ring at the end. (Of course, it's only speculation, but some say this is the reason Flatt and Scruggs finally broke up.)

Here's a Jimmy Martin style ending as you might play it on the last line of *John Henry*:

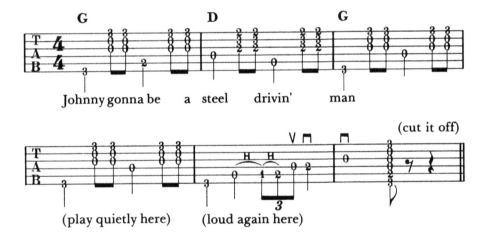

Listen to recordings to pick up some of the other beginnings and endings that are sometimes used for songs.

Endings for Instrumentals

On instrumental pieces, a two- or four-measure ending is tagged on after the last measure of the actual tune by the instrument that took the final break. It's patterned after the old "shave and a haircut: two bits" phrase:

Some of the following runs are double shave-and-a-haircut endings (four measures). You can play either half of the longer runs for a shorter, two-measure ending. Occasionally these are used for songs as well.

Good luck with this next batch of tunes!

Capo on 2nd fret:
actual Key of A

24 25

Old Joe Clark

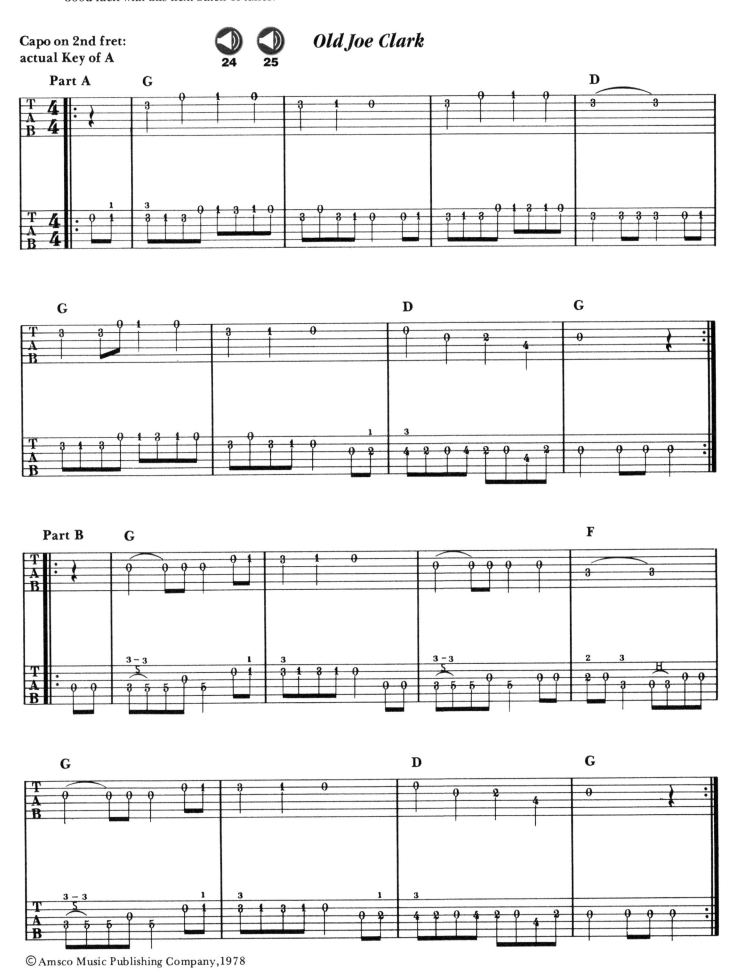

Soldier's Joy

Backup
(with simple bas runs)

Key of D

Part A

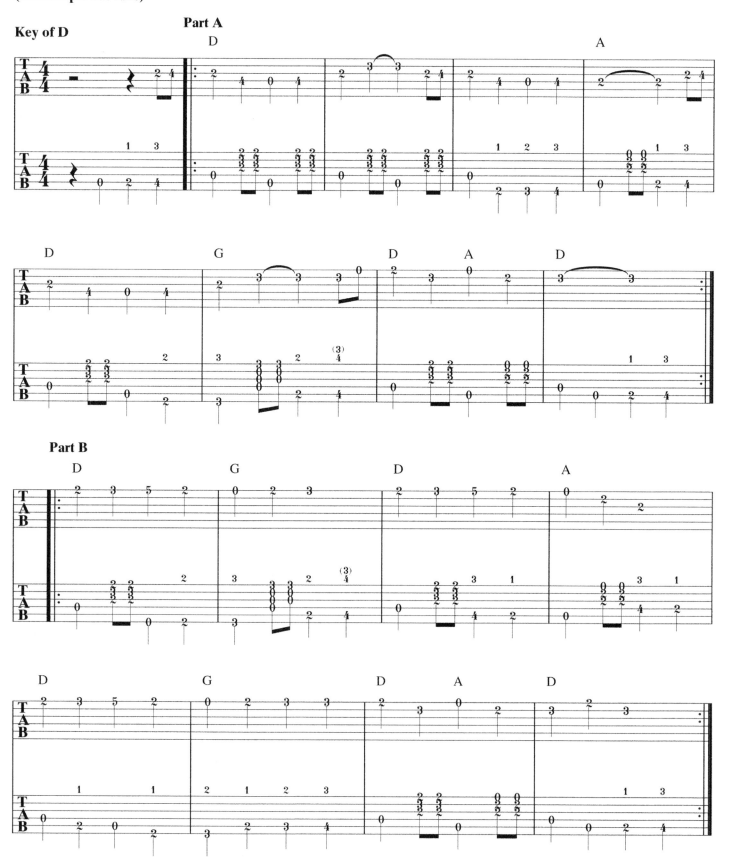

Soldier's Joy

Break

Cripple Creek

Capo on 2nd fret:
actual Key of A

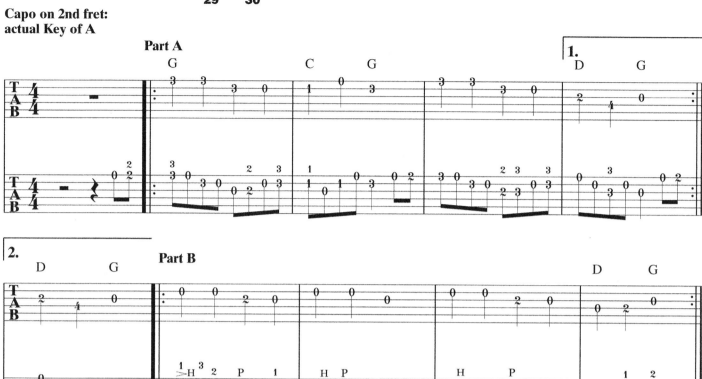

© Amsco Music Publishing Company, 1978

Fire on the Mountain

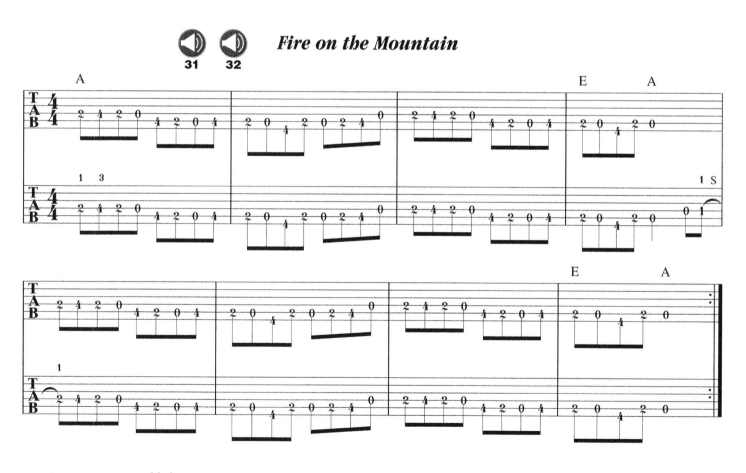

© Amsco Music Publishing Company, 1978

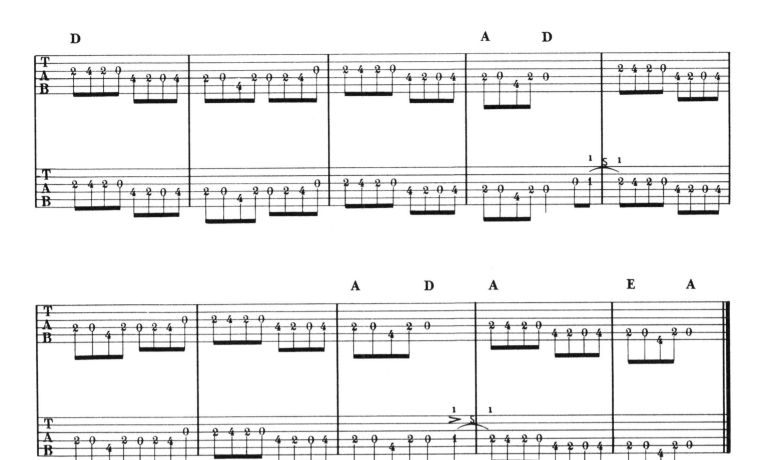

Salt Creek

**Capo on 2nd fret:
actual Key of A**

Bill Monroe and Bradford Keith

Part A

Blackberry Blossom

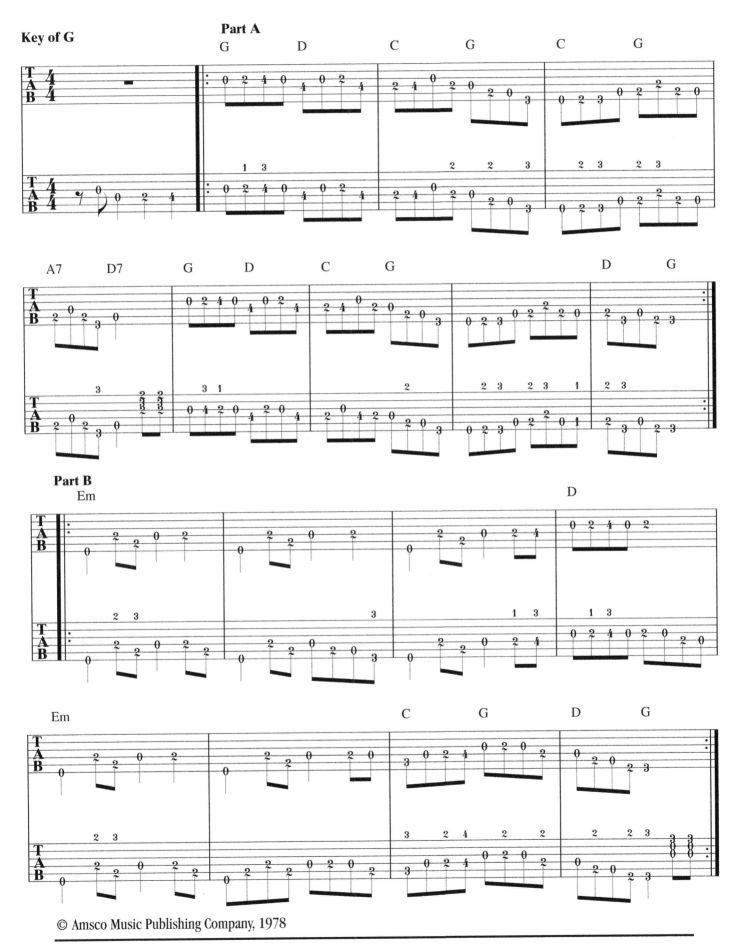

Key of G   Part A   37   38

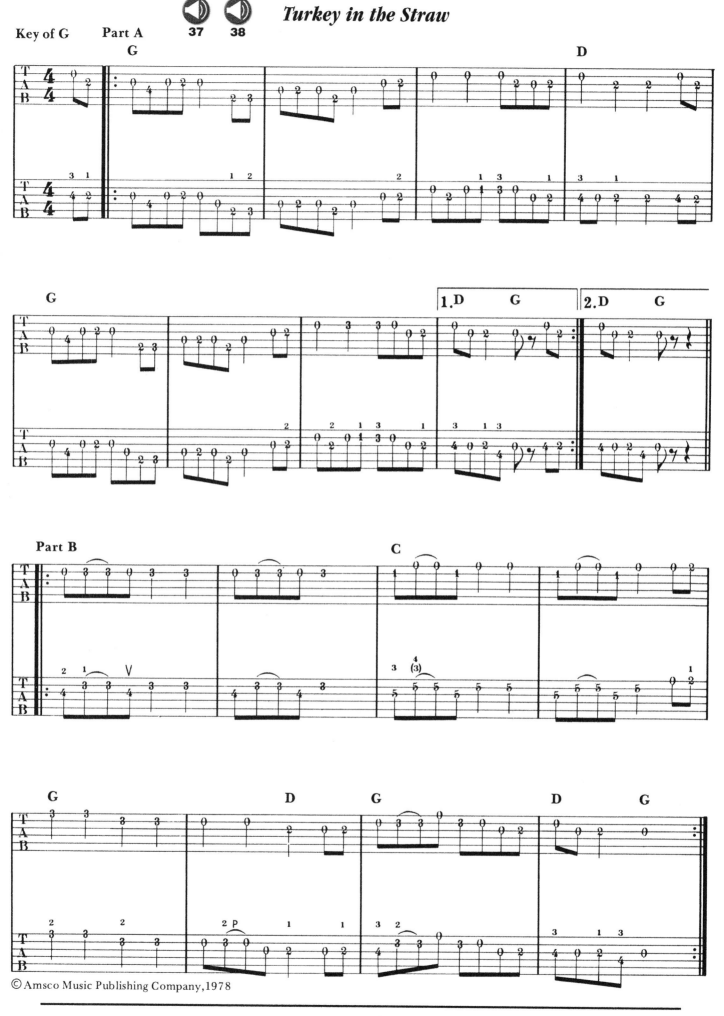

© Amsco Music Publishing Company, 1978

Nine Pound Hammer

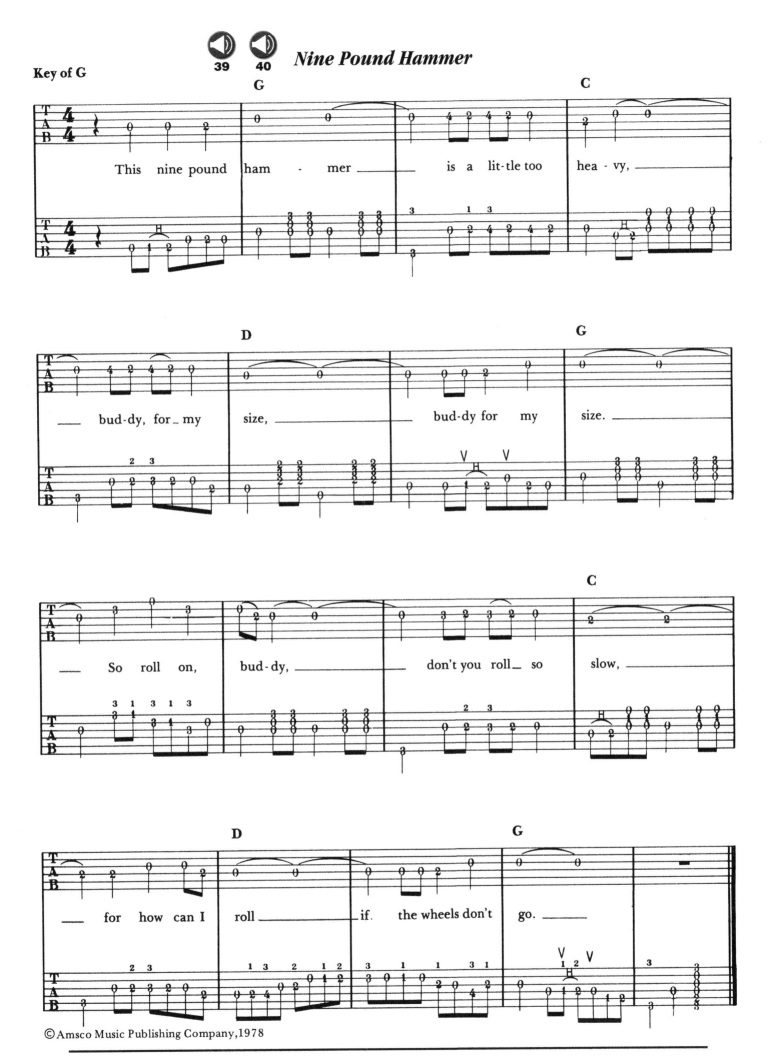

Sitting on Top of the World

Capo on 2nd fret:
actual Key of A
Backup
(advanced runs)

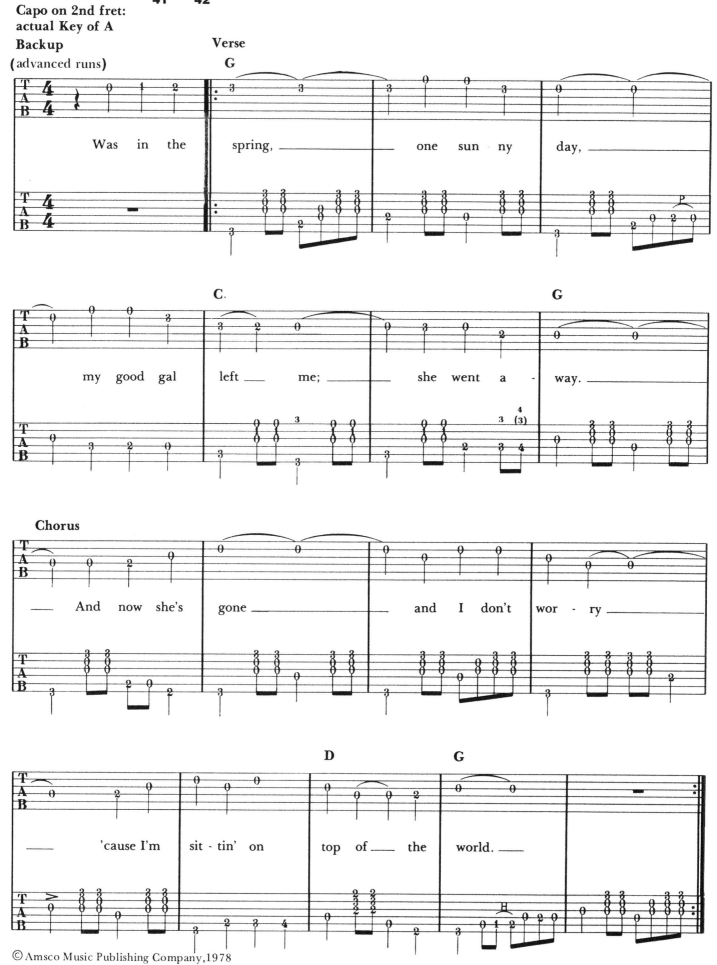

Sitting on Top of the World

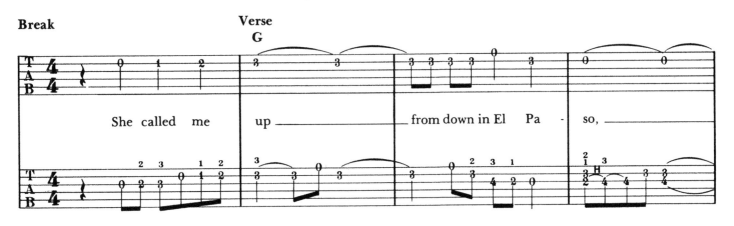

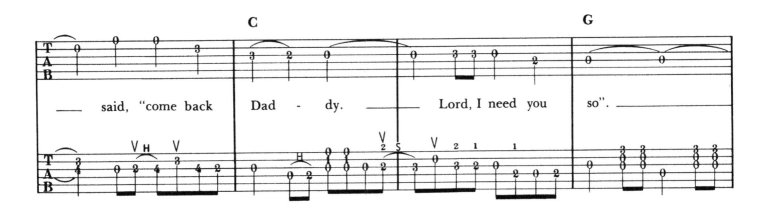

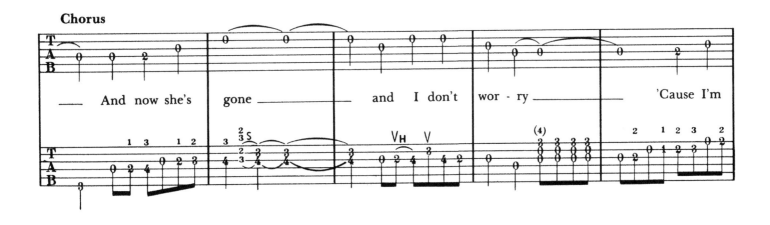

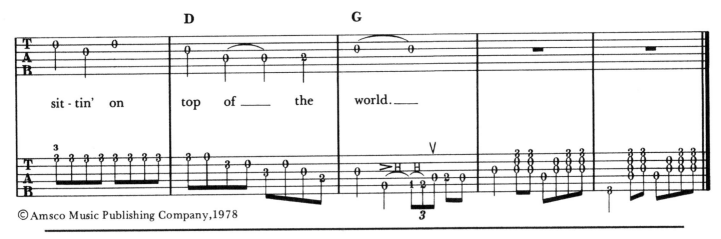

Footprints in the Snow

Backup
(advanced runs)

Key of E

© Amsco Music Publishing Company, 1978

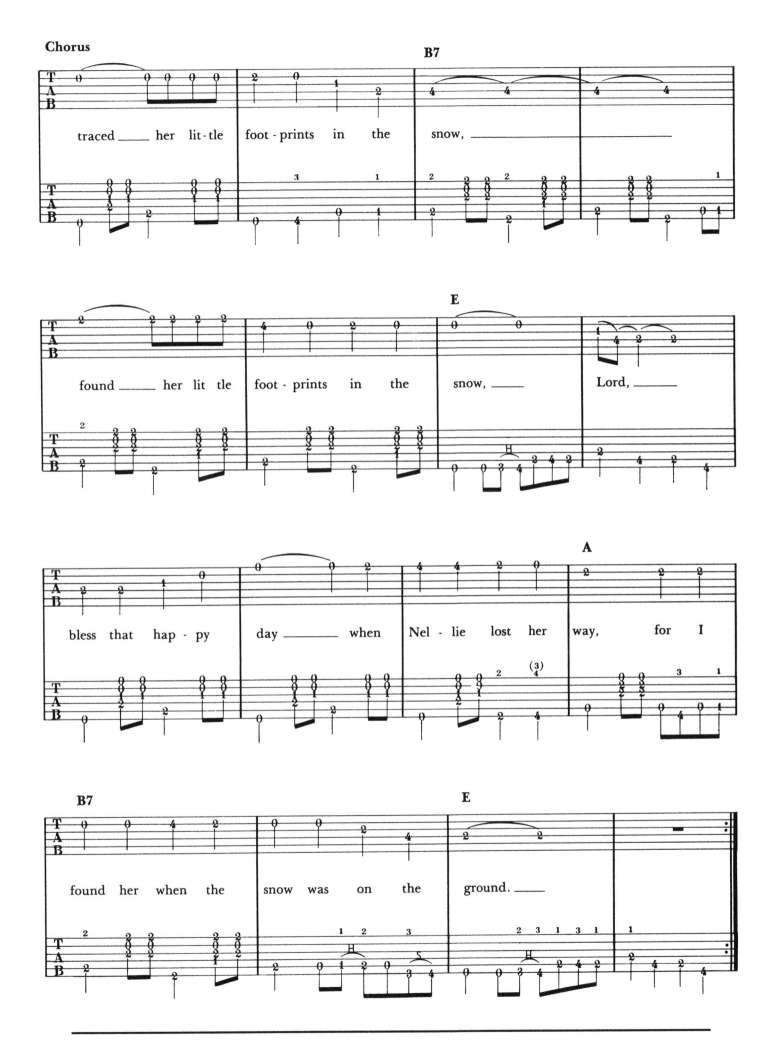

Footprints in the Snow

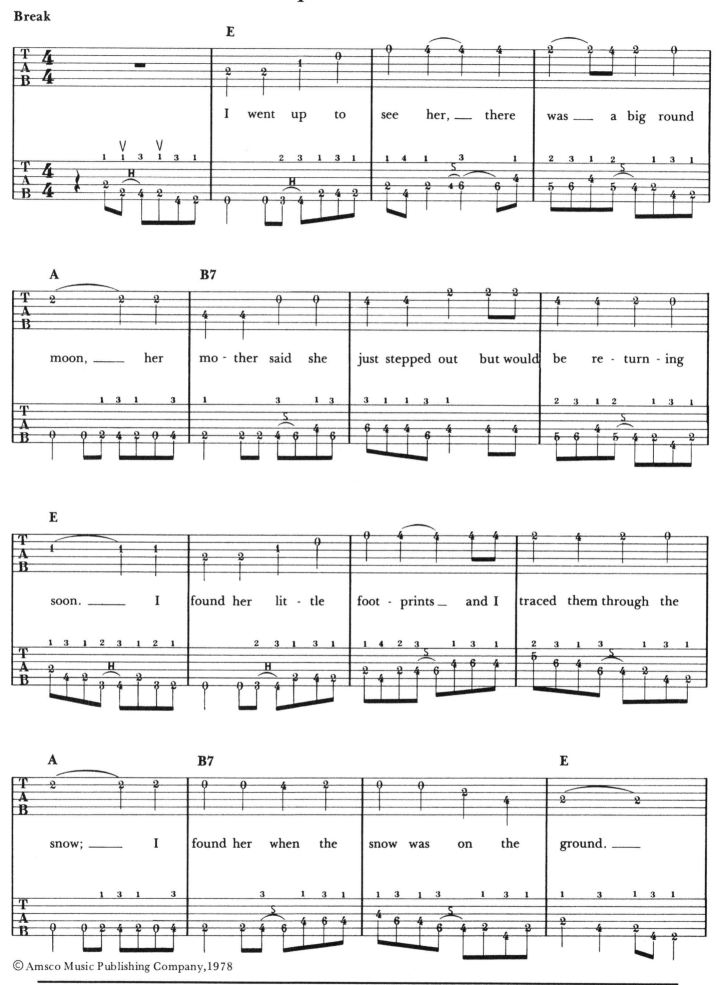

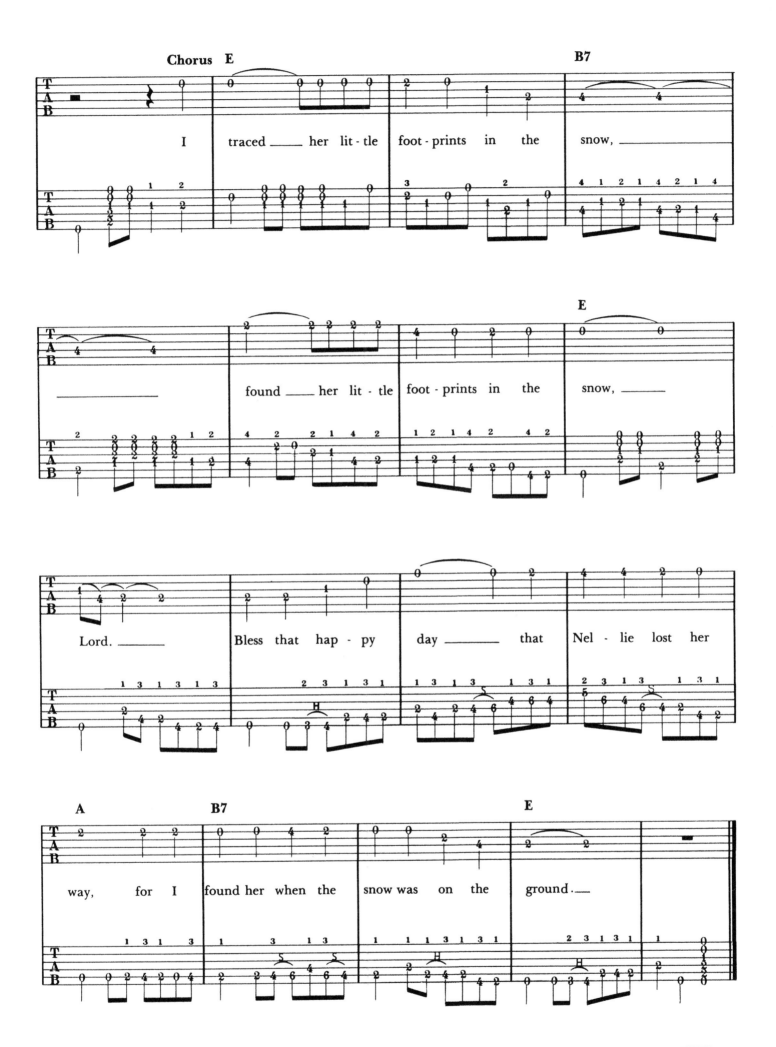

Little Maggie

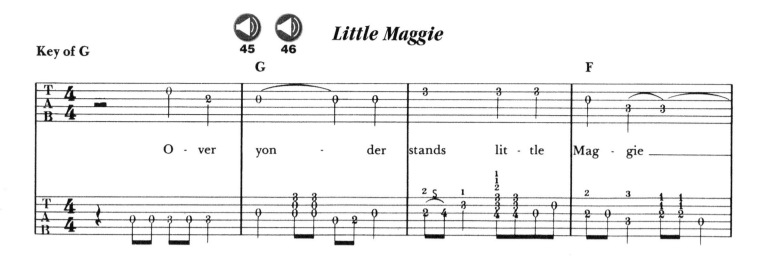

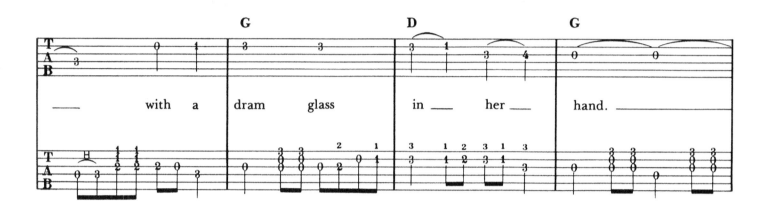

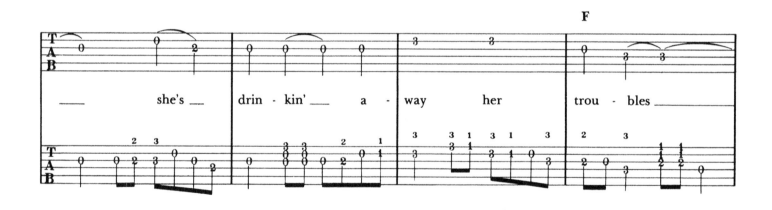

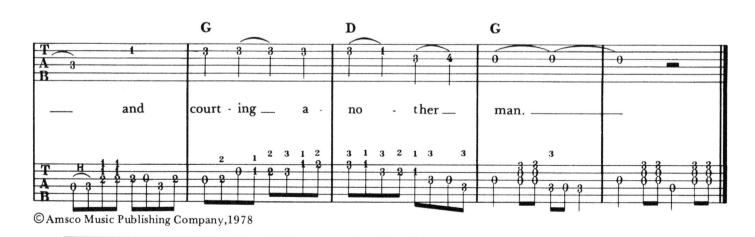

Some Advanced Flatpicking Techniques

Crosspicking

Crosspicking is a kind of playing in which you pick three neighboring strings in a repeated, rolling pattern. The style is derived from the mandolin playing of Jesse McReynolds (of Jim and Jesse), and it produces an effect similar to the sound of bluegrass banjo rolls. Crosspicking is dazzling in fast tunes but can be very gentle and pretty when used for texture in slower songs like *Dark Hollow.* Here's one example of a crosspicking pattern:

Here, the pick motion deviates from the normal down and up procedure. It's very difficult to master and will take a lot of practice, so don't get discouraged. If necessary, use a little extra wrist and hand motion to get it evened out. You can also play these passages with the normal, strictly alternating pick stroke. This approach is equally useful and gives a slightly different rhythmic effect.

The usual practice in crosspicking is to weave a melody into the pattern in the following way: rather than playing the same three notes the entire time, change notes on one or more of the strings as the picking pattern continues. For example:

(This can also be played with normal back - and - forth picking)

Melodic crosspicking is used in the breaks for *Dark Hollow* and *Live and Let Live.* When possible, let some notes ring as others are being played. You'll get a pleasing stringy effect with nice overlapping sonorities.

Many other three-string crosspicking variations are possible for different rhythmic and melodic purposes. Try these examples to get an idea of what can be done. Maybe in the future you can use some of these irregularities to fit particular melodies.

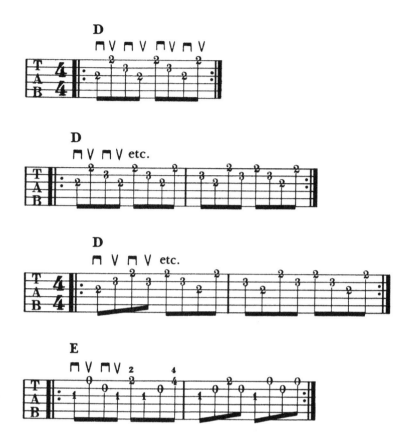

I use a pattern like this last one in my break to Tony Trischka's tune, *The Parson's Duck* on Country Cooking's *Barrel of Fun* (Rounder 0033). Also listen as much as possible to Clarence White, Jesse McReynolds, and others, to get acquainted with the style.

Syncopation and Unexpected Accents

The most important way to make your playing sound distinctive and accomplished is to develop a driving, solid sense of rhythm while incorporating interesting rhythmic surprises and deviations from the ever-present one-two, boom-chink-boom-chink of the bluegrass beat.

You can shake things up by accenting certain notes that fall on up-strokes of the pick. When you accent an up-stroke, you are putting emphasis on what is normally a weaker note. Shifting the accent to a weak subdivision of the beat is called syncopation. It often involves tied notes in which the note begins on the weak part of the beat (second eighth note) and is held over through the beginning (first eighth note) of the next beat. You've already used a mild form of syncopation in the second part of *Turkey in the Straw*. Here are a few examples of syncopation and accented up-strokes in backup playing. Also, watch for syncopation in the breaks for *Pretty Polly* and *John Henry.*

In the last examples, it's hard to resist playing a down-stroke on the third beat. But hold your horses and wait until the following eighth note. Then hit the D string with a firm up-stroke. This syncopation of the bass note really adds some interest to the basic backup strumming pattern. Be the first on your block to try it.

Used properly, syncopated notes can hit you by surprise and add delightful thrust to your music. Clarence White's masterful use of syncopation and unexpected accents is what makes his playing so exciting and unmistakable. The solo to *John Henry* is in Clarence's style. To help you put the right inflections in these breaks, listen to these invaluable records on which he is featured:

The Kentucky Colonels, *Appalachian Swing* (This is out of print, but try to find someone who's got it. It's a classic.)

The Kentucky Colonels, *1965–1967* Rounder 0070

The White Brothers, *Live in Sweden 1973* Rounder 0073 (The New Kentucky Colonels)

Chunking Chords and Left-Hand Damping

Chunking is a style of rhythm playing used for a very jaunty beat reminiscent of western swing music. Bluegrass mandolin players use it all the time for backup. Use movable chord forms that contain no open strings. Try the following using these chord forms:

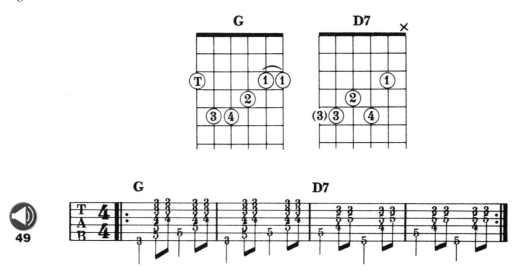

Play the first bass note as usual. Immediately after playing the down-strum, decrease the pressure of your left-hand fingers without removing them completely from the strings (hold the chord position). This is called left-hand damping. The chord will be abruptly cut off, producing a snappy, popping rhythmic sound. Make sure that the chord is actually sounded before you cut it off with your left hand. After the up-strum you really only hear a click on the strings, since the chord is not firmly fretted and actual notes will not ring. After the up-strum, re-apply the full pressure of your left hand and repeat the process starting with the next bass note.

Floating

One of the most recent styles, which has been developed by Tony Rice and other modern bluegrass guitarists, makes a unique of open strings. (Mike Scap, an excellent flatpicker from Colorado, dubbed it floating, which is pretty descriptive.) The technique is similar to Keith-style melodic banjo playing. Look for it in the break to *Live and Let Live*. It's tricky mostly for the right hand, since a note is often followed by a lower note on a higher string, or by a higher note on a lower string (if you can follow that!).

Once you've made it through this book, you should have no trouble learning songs on your own, and you'll certainly be ready to start making up your own breaks. I'm sure that experimenting with your own ideas will give you extra excitement and satisfaction when you play.

I'll leave you with this sage advice from Bill Monroe, who once said to me, "Boys, always keep lookin' for those new notes."

Pretty Polly

Key of G

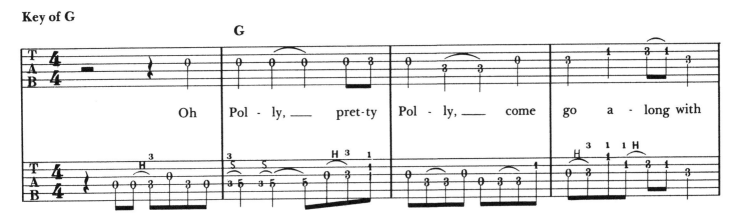

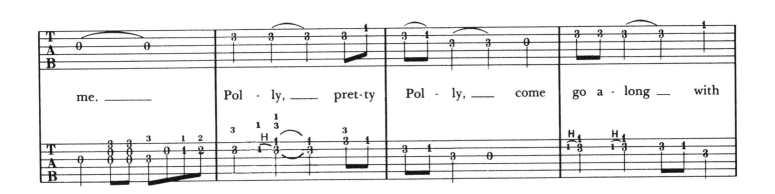

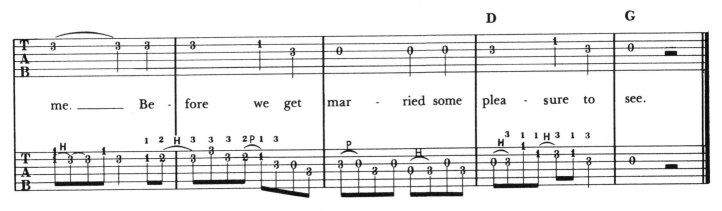

Farewell Blues

Capo on 2nd fret:
actual key of D

Ropollo, Pettis, Meyers, Schoebel

Part A

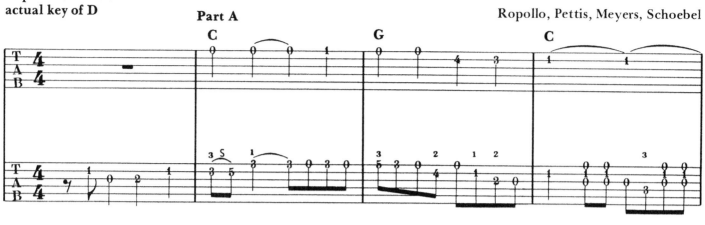

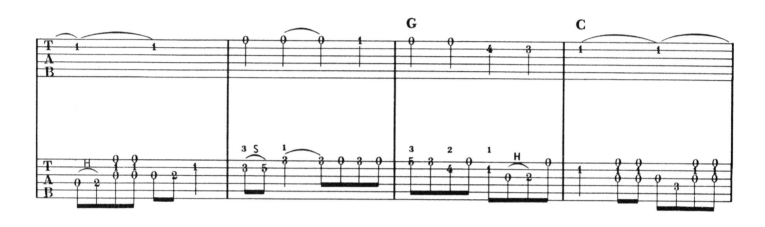

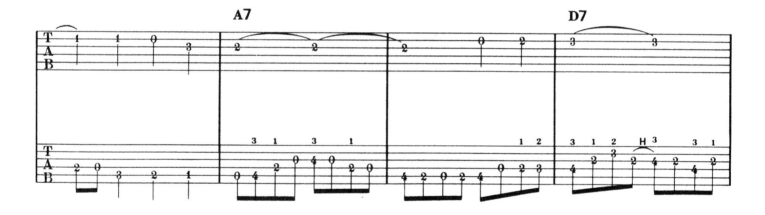

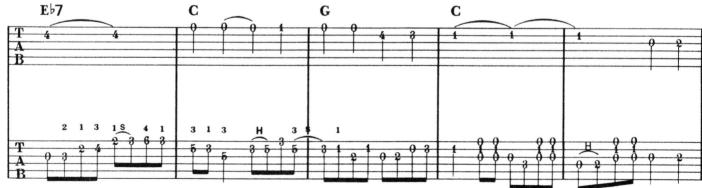

Part B

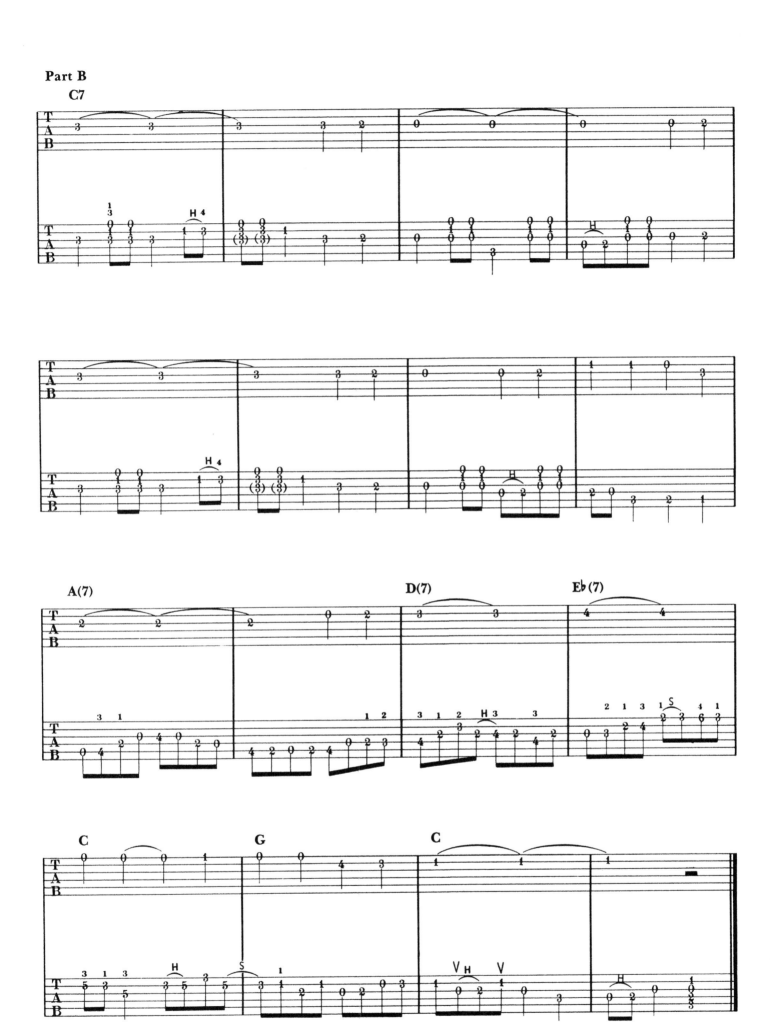

John Henry

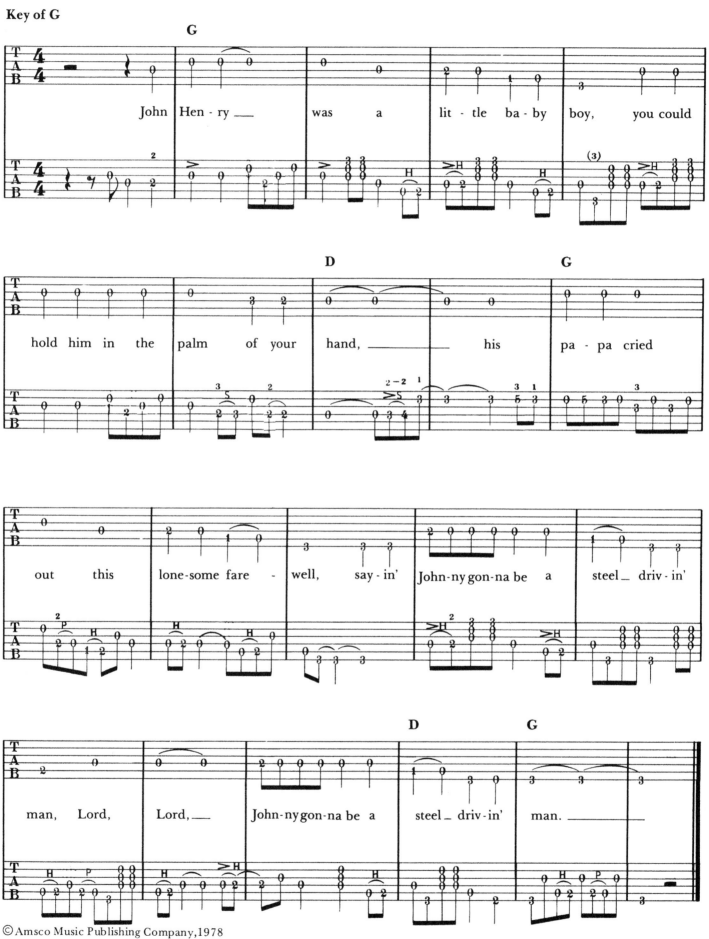

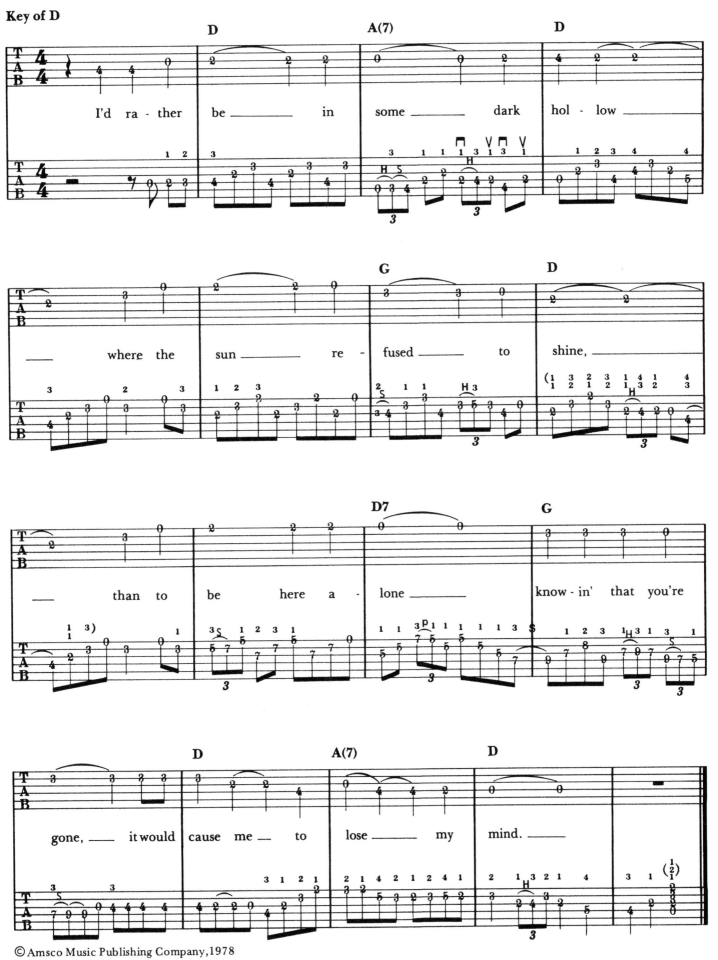

Live and Let Live

Capo on 4th fret:
actual Key of B

Wiley Walker and Gene Sullivan

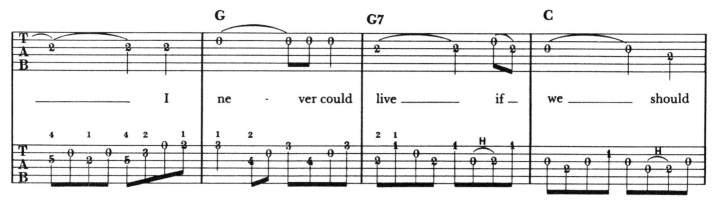

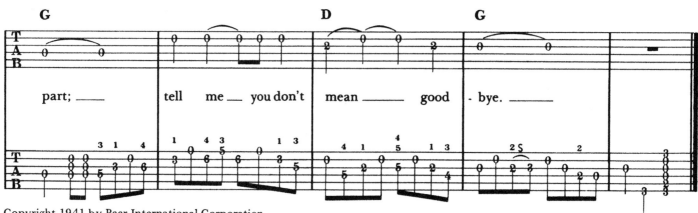

Appendices

Tuning

The music will be much more enjoyable for you and your audience if you keep your guitar properly tuned. So take all the time you need to tune it well.

Tune each string carefully to a piano, a guitar pitch pipe, or another instrument that's already in tune. Listen carefully to the reference note, and then to your note, and decide whether yours is too low or too high. Then tune it accordingly until they sound exactly the same. After you've tuned all the strings, play a few chords and listen for strings that don't sound quite right. Adjust them 'til you can play two or three different chords that sound in tune.

If you only have one note of reference (such as a tuning fork or one note from another instrument) you can tune your guitar like this:

Tune the one string to the reference note (say it's an A). Then tune the low E string until the note on the fifth fret matches the open A.

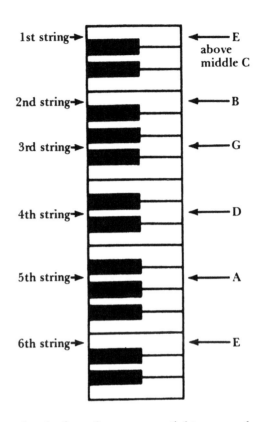

The fifth fret of the A string should match the open D.
The fifth fret of the D string should match the open G.
The fourth fret of the G string should match the open B.
The fifth fret of the B string should match the open E above it.

This method is not perfect, so when you're finished, play a few chords and make fine adjustments until things sound just right.

Don't let tuning frustrate you. It often takes a while to develop your ear so that you can hear the fine differences in pitch. When you're first learning, it's very helpful to have someone with an educated ear assist you. As you play more, always try to improve your own ability to hear pitch differences. Contrary to popular belief, this skill can be learned.

Chord Chart

G (Best Way)	G (optional)	G7	Gm
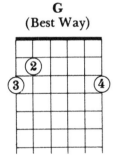	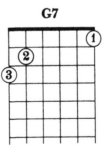	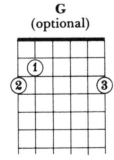	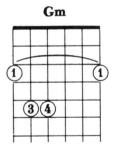

C	C	C7	Cm
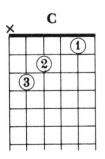	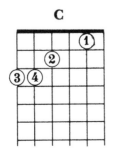	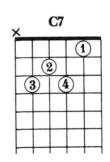	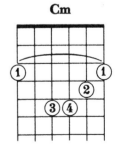

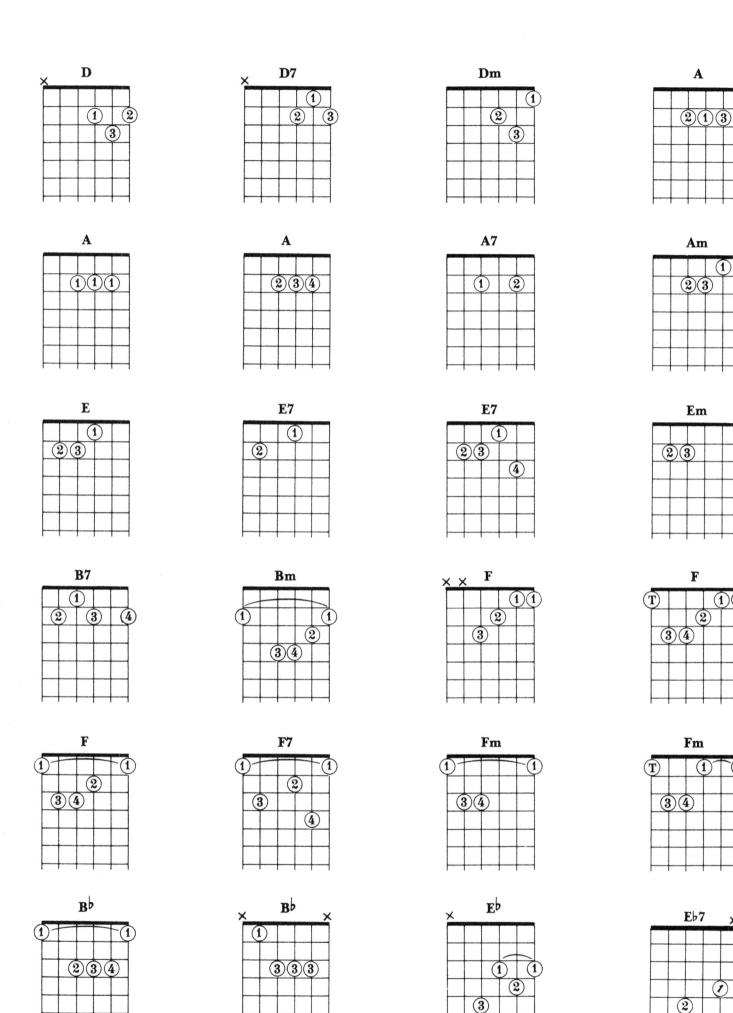

Different Keys, Transposition and the Use of a Capo

Transposition

In every key there are three primary chords commonly used in most bluegrass tunes. These are referred to as the I, IV, and V chords. In the key of G, they are G, C, and D, respectively. If you know a song in one key, you can play it in another key by substituting for each chord a corresponding chord in the new key.

This procedure is called transposition. For example, if you know *Cripple Creek* in G (chords G, C, and D) and want to play it in the key of A using A position chords, substitute an A chord for the G, a D chord for the C, and an E chord for the D. Here is a chart showing corresponding I, IV, and V chords for different keys. Within any key, V7 can be substituted for V (e.g., D7 instead of D in the key of G). Also shown are some other chords commonly found in bluegrass tunes.

THREE MAIN CHORDS

KEY	I	IV	V
G	G	C	D(7)
C	C	F	G(7)
A	A	D	E(7)
D	D	G	A(7)
E	E	A	B(7)

OTHER CHORDS

KEY	II or IIm	III or IIIm		VI or VIm		VIIb
G	A	Am	B	Bm	E	Em	F
C	D	Dm	E	Em	A	Am	Bb
A	B	Bm	C#	C#m	F#	F#m	G
D	E	Em	F#	F#m	B	Bm	C
E	F#	F#m	G#	G#m	C#	C#m	D

Using a Capo

An even more common way to change key in bluegrass music is to use a capo. If you know how to play a song in one key, a capo allows you to play it in several other keys as well, while using the same chord positions and fingerings. For example, if you play *Cripple Creek* in G chord positions with a capo on the second fret, you are actually playing in the key of A. Here is a chart showing the actual keys in which you will be playing if you are using a particular set of chord positions with the capo on different frets:

PLAY CHORD POSITIONS FOR:	ACTUAL KEY WITH CAPO:				
	on 1st fret	on 2nd fret	on 3rd fret	on 4th fret	on 5th fret
G	Ab	A	Bb	B	C
C	Db	D	Eb	E	F
A	Bb	B	C	Db	D
D	Eb	E	F	Gb(F#)	G
E	F	Gb(F#)	G	Ab	A

Here are some reasons for using a capo:

1) To match vocal range. Say you know a tune in G on the guitar, but you want to sing it higher. Use the capo to change to the key of A, B, or C, and raise the pitch to suit your voice.

2) To play in standard keys. Many fiddle tunes, bluegrass instrumentals, and some songs are played in standard keys almost all the time. If the tune is better suited to the guitar (for better soloing or particular backup effects) in different chord positions, use the capo to match the actual key of the tune. For example, *Old Joe Clark* is always played in the key of A on the fiddle or mandolin. It is usually played in G position on the guitar, so put the capo on the second fret and play in G. (The actual key is now A.)

3) Other musical considerations. You can control some aspects of how a song sounds by the chord positions you use and by the position of the capo (high or low) on the neck. Different chord positions have different characteristic sounds on the guitar. You'll certainly become familiar with them as you play more and more. Here is a decision you might make: *Wildwood Flower* is a sort of folky-sounding tune with an easy, rolling rhythm. If you want to play the song in the key of C, you would probably choose to play it in C position without a capo for a fuller, less biting sound. On the other hand, if you play *Live and Let Live* in the key of C, you would probably choose to play in G position with a capo on the fifth fret to get a more hard-driving bluegrass sound with punchy Flatt runs high on the neck.

Discography

Norman Blake
Natasha's Waltz (Rounder 11530)

Russ Barenberg with Country Cooking
Country Cooking: 26 Instrumentals (Rounder 11551)

Dan Crary
Guitar (Sugar Hill 3730)

Tony Rice with J.D. Crowe
J.D. Crowe & the New South (Rounder CD-0044)

Lester Flatt & Earl Scruggs
Blue Ridge Cabin Home (Rebel 102)

Jim & Jesse
1952-55 (Bear Family BCD-15635)

Jimmy Martin
You Don't Know My Mind (Rounder CD SS21)

Bill Monroe
Essential Bill Monroe 1945-49 (Columbia /Legacy C2K-52478)

Reno & Smiley
Early Years (King 7001)

Tony Rice
Tony Rice (Rounder CD-0085)

Doc Watson
Doc Watson (Vanguard VMD-79152)

Clarence White with The Kentucky Colonels
Appalachian Swing (Rounder CD-SS31)
Kentucky Colonels (Beat Goes On 357)

If you have any trouble finding any of these CDs write to:

Rounder Records
1 Camp Street
Cambridge, MA 02140
1-800-ROUNDER

County Sales
P.O. Box 191
Floyd, VA 24091